Issues
for Today

Third Edition

Reading For Today Series, Book 3

LORRAINE C. SMITH

Adelphi University

NANCY NICI MARE

English Language Institute
Queens College
The City University of New York

THOMSON
HEINLE

Australia • Canada • Mexico • Singapore • United Kingdom • United States

THOMSON

™

HEINLE

Issues for Today, Third Edition
Lorraine C. Smith and Nancy Nici Mare

Publisher, Adult and Academic ESL: *James W. Brown*
Senior Acquisitions Editor: *Sherrise Roehr*
Director of Development: *Anita Raducanu*
Development Editor: *Sarah Barnicle*
Editorial Assistant: *Audra Longert*
Senior Production Editor: *Maryellen E. Killeen*
Senior Marketing Manager: *Charlotte Sturdy*
Director, Global ESL Training & Development:
  Evelyn Nelson
Senior Print Buyer: *Mary Beth Hennebury*

Contributing Writer: *Barbara Gaffney*
Compositor: *Parkwood Composition Service*
Project Manager: *Hockett Editorial Service*
Photo Researcher: *Susan Van Etten*
Photography Manager: *Sheri Blaney*
Illustrator: *Glenn Reid*
Cover Designer: *Ha Ngyuen*
Text Designer: *Carole Rollins*
Printer: *Quebecor World*

Printed in the United States of America
1 2 3 4 5 6 7 8 9 10   06 05 04 03

For more information contact Heinle, 25 Thomson Place, Boston, Massachusetts 02210 USA, or you can visit our Internet site at http://www.heinle.com

For permission to use material from this text or product contact us:
Tel   1-800-730-2214
Fax   1-800-730-2215
Web   www.thomsonrights.com

Library of Congress Control Number   2003107157

ISBN   0-88377-112-8
ISE ISBN   1413000789

CREDITS

To Joseph

ACKNOWLEDGMENTS

We are grateful to everyone at Heinle, especially to Sherrise Roehr for her continued support, to Sarah Barnicle for her keen eye and untiring efforts, and to Maryellen Killeen for her hard work. Special thanks also go to Rachel Youngman of Hockett Editorial Service for her diligence. As always, we are appreciative of the ongoing encouragement from our family and friends.

L.C.S. and N.N.M.

CONTENTS

Unit	Chapter and Title	Reading Skills Focus	Structure Focus	Follow-up Activities Skills Focus
CNN® Video Report and Internet Topics				
Unit 1 Trends in Living	Chapter 1 **A Cultural Difference: Being on Time** *Page 2*	• Preview reading through title and prereading questions • Understand True/False, Multiple Choice, Short Answer questions • Use context clues to understand and use vocabulary • Identify main ideas and details • Organize information using an outline • Use outline to recall and summarize information	• Identify and compare parts of speech in context: nouns, verbs, and adjectives • Recognize nouns by the suffixes: *-ing* and *-ation* • Use singular and plural nouns; affirmative and negative verb forms appropriately in sentences	• *Speaking:* Express opinions supported by examples; predict • *Writing:* Write a journal entry; React personally to a reading; Use a graphic organizer to develop ideas
	Chapter 2 **Changing Lifestyles and New Eating Habits** *Page 20*	• Preview reading through title and prereading questions • Understand True/False, Multiple Choice, Short Answer questions • Use context clues to understand and use vocabulary • Identify main ideas and details • Organize information using a flowchart • Use flowchart to recall and summarize information • Read and interpret bar graphs • Make inferences • Assert opinions	• Identify and compare parts of speech in context: nouns, verbs, and adjectives • Recognize the suffix: *-er* • Use singular and plural nouns; affirmative and negative verb forms appropriately in sentences	• *Listening:* Share information and support opinions by example • *Writing:* Write an explanatory paragraph using description and examples; Write a journal entry expressing likes and dislikes; Use a graphic organizer to list ideas
• *Listening and Viewing:* **CNN® Video Report:** Nutrition Survey *Page 58* • *Viewing and Research:* **Internet Search:** USDA Food Pyramid *Page 58*	Chapter 3 **Dreams: Making Them Work for Us** *Page 37*	• Preview reading through title and prereading questions • Understand True/False, Multiple Choice, Short Answer questions • Use context clues to understand vocabulary • Identify main ideas and details • Organize information using an outline • Use outline to recall and summarize information	• Identify parts of speech from context: adjectives and nouns; verbs and nouns • Recognize the suffix: *-ness* • Use the simple present tense	• *Listening:* Develop interview questions and conduct an interview • *Writing:* Write a journal entry expressing likes and dislikes

Unit	Chapter and Title	Reading Skills Focus	Structure Focus	Follow-up Activities Skills Focus
CNN® Video Report and Internet Topics				
Unit 2 **Issues In Society**	Chapter 4 **Language: Is It Always Spoken?** *Page 60*	• Use prereading questions to activate background knowledge • Preview illustrations and title to aid comprehension • Understand True/False, Multiple Choice, Short Answer questions • Skim reading for main idea • Scan for information • Use context clues to understand vocabulary • Organize information using an outline • Use outline to recall and summarize information • Choose correct dictionary definitions	• Identify parts of speech in context: nouns, adjectives, and verbs • Use past, present, or future verb tenses in the affirmative or negative form • Recognize the suffixes: *-in* , *-t*, and *-ct* and use them correctly	• *Discussion:* Describe nonverbal communication; Research ASL and discuss results • *Writing:* Write a brief biography of a famous person with hearing loss; Write a journal entry about learning sign language; List advantages and disadvantages of the choice to remain non-hearing or deaf
	Chapter 5 **Loneliness: How Can We Overcome It?** *Page 75*	• Use prereading questions to activate background knowledge • Preview illustration and title to aid comprehension • Understand True/False, Multiple Choice, Short Answer questions • Use context clues to understand vocabulary • Skim reading for main idea and scan for important details • Organize information using a flowchart • Use flowchart to recall and summarize information • Make inferences • Choose correct dictionary definitions	• Identify parts of speech in context: nouns, adjectives, and verbs • Use singular or plural nouns as required by context • Recognize the suffixes: *-ness* and *-ity* and use them correctly	• *Discussion:* Discuss causes of loneliness and research on the subject; Discuss result with class about survey • *Writing:* Write a journal entry about loneliness; Take a survey about loneliness
• *Listening and Viewing:* **CNN® Video Report:** Grandparents as Parents *Page 112* • *Viewing and Research:* **Internet Search:** Sign Language *Page 112*	Chapter 6 **The Importance of Grandmothers** *Page 90*	• Use prereading questions to activate background knowledge • Preview title to predict reading topic • Understand True/False, Multiple Choice, Short Answer questions • Skim reading for main idea • Scan for supporting details • Make inferences • Organize information using a flowchart • Use flowchart to recall and summarize information • Use context clues to understand vocabulary • Read and interpret data in pie and bar charts	• Identify parts of speech in context: nouns, verbs, and adjectives • Recognize the suffixes: *-tion* and *-ce* • Use the affirmative or negative of a past, present, or future verb tense • Use singular and plural forms of nouns	• *Discussion:* Make comparisons about grandmothers and discuss reasons for opinions; Discuss unit themes and support ideas with examples • *Writing:* Conduct a survey and record answers in a chart; Write a journal entry about the treatment of grandchildren

SKILLS

SKILLS

Unit	Chapter and Title	Reading Skills Focus	Structure Focus	Follow-up Activities Skills Focus
CNN® Video Report and Internet Topics				
Unit 4 **Science and History**	Chapter 10 **Ancient Artifacts and Ancient Air** *Page 176*	• Use background knowledge to understand reading through prereading questions • Understand True/False, Multiple Choice, Short Answer questions • Scan reading for main idea • Use context clues to understand vocabulary • Take notes and organize information using an outline • Use outline to recall and summarize information • Select accurate dictionary definitions	• Use parts of speech correctly in context: nouns, verbs, adjectives, and conjunctions • Use the affirmative or negative forms of the past, present, and future verb tenses • Recognize the suffixes: *-ion, -ation,* and *-y* and use them correctly	• *Discussion:* Discuss issues regarding the discoveries and ethics of archeology • *Writing:* Make plans about a hypothetical archeological situation in a group and compare plans with other groups; Write a journal entry about an archeological decision
	Chapter 11 **How Lunar Eclipses Have Changed History** *Page 195*	• Preview chapter through title, diagram, and questions • Understand True/False, Multiple Choice, Short Answer questions • Use context clues to understand vocabulary • Scan reading for main ideas • Take notes and organize information using a chart • Use chart to recall and summarize information • Select accurate dictionary definitions	• Use parts of speech correctly in context: nouns, verbs, adjectives, and adverbs • Use the singular or plural forms of nouns • Recognize the suffixes: *-ity* and *-ous* and use them correctly	• *Discussion:* Discuss superstitions and beliefs in small group • *Writing:* Write a journal entry about personal superstitions; Write a list about superstitions and compare with others; Describe a solar eclipse
• *Listening and Viewing:* **CNN® Video Report:** Water on Mars? *Page 236* • *Viewing and Research:* **Internet Search:** The Planet Mars/Lunar Eclipses *Page 236*	Chapter 12 **Mars: Our Neighbor in Space** *Page 214*	• Preview photo and chapter art • Use prereading questions to activate background knowledge and predict topic of reading • Understand True/False, Multiple Choice, Short Answer questions • Use context clues to understand vocabulary • Scan reading for the main idea • Organize information using an outline • Use outline to recall and summarize information • Choose accurate dictionary definitions	• Identify parts of speech in context: nouns, adjectives, and verbs • Recognize the suffixes: *-al* and *-ify* and use them correctly • Use singular and plural forms of nouns • Use the affirmative or negative forms of the past, present, and future verb tenses	• *Discussion:* Discuss opinions about extraterrestrial life; Compare space programs in different countries; Discuss technology and support opinions with examples • *Writing:* Research quantitative and qualitative details about other planets in the solar system; Record details in lists on a chart; Compare charts with other classmates'; Write a journal entry about your opinion of life on other planets
		Index of Key Words and Phrases *Pages 237–238* **Skills Index** *Pages 239–240*		

PREFACE

Issues for Today, Third Edition, is a reading skills textbook intended for intermediate, academically oriented students of English as a second or foreign language. The passages in this thematically organized book introduce students to topics of universal interest. As students work with the materials in each chapter, they develop the kinds of extensive and intensive reading skills they will need to achieve academic success in English.

Issues for Today is one in a series of five reading skills texts. The complete series has been designed to meet the needs of students from the beginning to the advanced levels and includes the following:

- *Themes for Today*   beginning
- *Insights for Today*   high beginning
- *Issues for Today*   intermediate
- *Concepts for Today*   high intermediate
- *Topics for Today*   advanced

Issues for Today, Third Edition, consists of four thematic units. Each unit contains three chapters that deal with related subjects. At the same time, each chapter is independent, entirely separate in content from the other two chapters contained in that unit. This gives the instructor the option of either completing entire units or choosing individual chapters as a focus in class.

All of the chapters provide the students with interesting and stimulating topics to read, think about, discuss, and write about. The initial exercises are an introduction to each reading passage and encourage the students to think about the ideas, facts, and vocabulary that will be presented. The exercises that follow the reading passage are intended to improve reading comprehension skills as well as comprehension of English sentence structure. The activities will help them see relationships between parts of a sentence, between sentences, and between and within paragraphs. The articles contain useful vocabulary that the students can use in the real world and the exercises are designed to sharpen their ability to learn vocabulary from context. Students should learn not to rely on a bilingual dictionary. A word form exercise is included in each chapter to help students develop a "feel" for the patterns of word forms in English and an awareness of morphemes; for example, the suffix *-tion* always indicates a noun. Many vocabulary and word form selections are repeated in subsequent chapters to provide reinforcement.

The progression of exercises and activities in each chapter leads the students through general comprehension of main ideas, specific information, understanding structural details, and specific vocabulary. Since reading college material also involves note-taking skills, students are trained to organize the article via diagrams, charts, and outlines, and to briefly summarize the passage. Finally, the students practice manipulating new vocabulary by working with different parts of speech, and varying the tense in both affirmative and negative forms, and singular and plural forms.

Issues for Today, Third Edition, contains a Prereading Preparation section, which contains thoughtful, motivating questions and activities. The third edition includes improved graphics and new photographs, which are accompanied by questions designed to enhance students' comprehension of information presented. The Information Organization exercise includes outlines, charts, and flowcharts, depending on each reading and the type of information it contains. This organization of information section will make the Reading Recall a more purposeful activity. Furthermore, the Information Organization design takes into account students' different learning and organizational styles. The Follow-Up Activities section contains a variety of activities and provides opportunities for discussion and interaction. Moreover, *Issues for Today, Third Edition,* contains surveys, which provide students with the means and the opportunity to go out into the "real world" and interact with native English speakers in meaningful ways, and affords them the opportunity to collect data that they can bring back to class and combine, generating graphs of their own for interpretation and discussion. *Issues for Today, Third Edition,* includes end-of-unit crossword puzzles, which provide a review of the vocabulary encountered in all three chapters of each unit, and Unit Discussion questions, which help students think about, discuss, and make connections among the topics in the chapters of each unit.

New to the Third Edition

While most reading topics and activities in *Issues for Today, Third Edition,* remain from the previous edition, the authors have made several significant changes to this edition. The third edition contains two new chapters: "The Importance of Grandmothers" in the Issues in Society unit and "Solving Crime with Modern Technology" in the Justice and Crime unit.

In addition to the new chapters, the third edition is now accompanied by audio cassette tapes or CDs on which all the readings are recorded, as well as a theme-based CNN® video composed of clips, which complement the topic of one chapter in each unit. In the third edition of *Issues for Today,* video activities are found at the end of each unit to assist students in their viewing comprehension. Also new to *Issues for Today, Third Edition,* are Internet activities designed to encourage students with school or home access to the Internet to learn more about a topic they read about in their text.

These revisions and enhancements to *Issues for Today, Third Edition,* have been designed to help students improve their reading skills and develop confidence as they work through the text. At the same time, the third edition is structured so that the students will steadily progress toward skillful, independent reading. All of these activities are presented to prepare students for academic work and the world of information they will encounter.

INTRODUCTION

How to Use This Book

Each chapter in this book consists of the following:

Prereading Preparation
Reading Passage
Fact-Finding Exercise
Reading Analysis
Information Organization
Information Recall and Summary
Word Forms
Vocabulary in Context
Topics for Discussion and Writing
Follow-up Activities
CLOZE Quiz

Chapters 7–12 also include a Dictionary Skill exercise. Each unit contains a cross-word puzzle, which incorporates vocabulary from all three chapters in the unit. The discussion section at the end of each unit ties in the related topics of the three chapters. There are CNN® video and Internet activities at the end of each unit as well as an Index of Key Words and Phrases at the end of the book.

Prereading Preparation

This prereading activity is designed to stimulate student interest and provide preliminary vocabulary for the passage itself. The importance of prereading preparation should not be underestimated. Studies have shown the positive effect of prereading preparation in motivating student interest, activating background knowledge, and enhancing reading comprehension. Time should be spent describing and discussing the photographs and illustrations as well as discussing the chapter title and the prereading questions. Furthermore, students should try to relate the topic to their own experiences and try to predict what they are going to read about.

Reading Passage

The students will read the passage for the first time. They should be instructed to time themselves and to try to aim for a higher reading speed the second time they read the passage. They should also be encouraged to read *ideas*, not just words.

Fact-Finding Exercise

After reading the passage again, the students will read the True/False statements and check whether they are true or false. If the statement is false, the students will rewrite the statement so that it is true. They will then go back to the passage and find the line(s) that contain the correct answer. This activity can be done individually or in groups.

Reading Analysis

The students will read each question and answer it. The first question in this section always refers to the main idea. There are three possible answers. Two answers are incorrect because they are too general or too narrow, they are not mentioned in the passage, or they are false. When going over the exercise, the teacher should discuss with the students why the other two answers are incorrect. The rest of this exercise requires the students to think about the structure of the sentences and paragraphs, and the relationships of ideas to one another. This exercise is very effective when done in groups. It may also be done individually, but if done in groups it gives the students an excellent opportunity to discuss possible answers.

Information Organization

In this exercise, the students are asked to read the passage again, take notes, and organize the information they have just read. They may be asked to complete an outline, a table, or a flowchart. The teacher may want to review the concept of notetaking before beginning the exercise. The outline, table, or flowchart can be sketched on the blackboard by the teacher or a student and completed by individual students in front of the class. Variations can be discussed by the class as a group. It should be pointed out to students that in American colleges, teachers often base their exams on the notes that the students are expected to take during class lectures, and that they, too, will be tested on their notes.

Information Recall and Summary

The questions in this exercise are based on the notes the students took in the Information Organization exercise. Students should be instructed to read the questions and then to refer to their notes to answer them. They are also asked to write a summary of the article. The teacher may want to review how to summarize at the beginning of the class. This section can be prepared in class and discussed. Alternately, it can be assigned for homework.

Word Forms

As an introduction to the word form exercises in this book, it is recommended that the teacher first review parts of speech, especially verbs, nouns, adjectives, and adverbs. Teachers should point out each word form's position in a sentence. Students will develop a sense for which part of speech is missing in a given sentence. Teachers should also point out clues to tense and number, and whether an idea is affirmative or negative. Each section has its own instructions, depending on the particular pattern that is being introduced. For example, in the section containing words which take *-tion* in the noun form, the teacher can explain that in this exercise the student will look at the verb and noun forms of two types of words that use the suffix *-tion* in their noun form. (1) Some words simply add *-tion* to the verb: *convict/conviction;* if the word ends in *e*, the *e* is dropped first: *execute/execution;* (2) other words can drop the final *e* and add *-ation: combine/ combination.* This exercise is very effective when done in pairs. After students have a working knowledge of this type of exercise, it can be assigned for homework.

Dictionary Skills

This exercise, in Chapters 7–12, provides students with much-needed practice in selecting the appropriate dictionary entry for an unknown word, depending on the context. Students are given entries from Heinle's *Newbury House Dictionary.* The sentence containing the dictionary word is provided above the entry. After selecting the appropriate entry, the student rewrites the sentence using the chosen definition. The students should write the answer in a grammatically correct form, as they may not always be able to copy verbatim from the dictionary. The students can work in pairs on this exercise and report back to the class. They should be prepared to justify their choices.

Vocabulary in Context

This is a fill-in exercise designed as a review of the items in the previous exercises. This vocabulary has been covered either in the questions or the Reading Analysis section. It can be done for homework as a review or in class as group work.

Topics for Discussion and Writing

In this section, students are encouraged to use the information and vocabulary from the passage both orally and in writing. The writing assignment may be done in class or at home. There is a **Write in your journal** suggestion for every chapter. Students should be encouraged to keep a journal and respond to these questions. The teacher may want to read and respond to the students' journal entries, but not correct them.

Follow-Up Activities

This section contains various activities appropriate to the information in the passages. Some activities are designed for pair and small-group work. Students are encouraged to use the information and vocabulary from the passages both orally and in writing. The teacher may also use these questions and activities as home or in-class assignments.

CLOZE

The CLOZE quiz tests not only vocabulary, but also sentence structure and comprehension in general. The quiz is a modified version of the reading passage itself, with 20 items to be completed. At the top of the answer page, students are given the 20 words to be filled in the blank spaces. The quiz is placed at the end of each chapter. The quizzes can be done either as a test or as a group assignment.

CNN® Video Report and Internet Activities

At the end of each unit are optional activities designed to accompany one of the topics presented in each unit. The authentic CNN videos were chosen to expand on concepts presented in the readings, to reinforce vocabulary learned, and to encourage individual interest as well as group discussion. The optional Internet activities provide encouragement to students to explore information learned in *Issues for Today* through the technology available to them at school, in the library and computer labs, and at home.

Index of Key Words and Phrases

This section contains words and phrases from all the chapters for easy reference. It is located after the last chapter.

UNIT 1

TRENDS IN LIVING

A Cultural Difference: Being on Time

Prereading Preparation

1. What does **on time** mean?

2. Is it always important to be on time? Look at the table on page 3. How important is it to be on time for each appointment? Put a check mark in the box to show your answer. Discuss your answers with the class.

How Important Is It to Be on Time?				
Type of Appointment	Scheduled Time	Very Important	Slightly Important	Not Important
dentist	9 A.M.			
university class	11 A.M.			
lunch with a friend at school	12 P.M.			
dinner with your spouse	7 P.M.			
a friend's party	9 P.M.			
job interview in a bank	2 P.M.			

3. Are you usually on time, or are you usually late? Why?

4. Read the title of the article. What do you think this article is about?

A Cultural Difference: Being On Time

1   In the United States, it is important to be on time, or punctual, for an
2 appointment, a class, a meeting, etc. However, this may not be true in all
3 countries. An American professor discovered this difference while teaching a
4 class in a Brazilian university. The two-hour class was scheduled to begin at 10
5 A.M. and end at 12 P.M. On the first day, when the professor arrived on time, no
6 one was in the classroom. Many students came after 10 A.M. Several arrived after
7 10:30 A.M. Two students came after 11 A.M. Although all the students greeted the
8 professor as they arrived, few apologized for their lateness. Were these students
9 being rude? He decided to study the students' behavior.
10   The professor talked to American and Brazilian students about lateness in
11 both an informal and a formal situation: lunch with a friend and in a university
12 class, respectively. He gave them an example and asked them how they would
13 react. If they had a lunch appointment with a friend, the average American
14 student defined lateness as 19 minutes after the agreed time. On the other hand,
15 the average Brazilian student felt the friend was late after 33 minutes.

16 In an American university, students are expected to arrive at the appointed
17 hour. In contrast, in Brazil, neither the teacher nor the students always arrive at
18 the appointed hour. Classes not only begin at the scheduled time in the United
19 States, but they also end at the scheduled time. In the Brazilian class, only a few
20 students left the class at noon; many remained past 12:30 to discuss the class and
21 ask more questions. While arriving late may not be very important in Brazil,
22 neither is staying late.

23 The explanation for these differences is complicated. People from Brazilian
24 and North American cultures have different feelings about lateness. In Brazil, the
25 students believe that a person who usually arrives late is probably more
26 successful than a person who is always on time. In fact, Brazilians expect a
27 person with status or prestige to arrive late, while in the United States lateness
28 is usually considered to be disrespectful and unacceptable. Consequently, if a
29 Brazilian is late for an appointment with a North American, the American may
30 misinterpret the reason for the lateness and become angry.

31 As a result of his study, the professor learned that the Brazilian students
32 were not being disrespectful to him. Instead, they were simply behaving in the
33 appropriate way for a Brazilian student in Brazil. Eventually, the professor was
34 able to adapt his own behavior so that he could feel comfortable in the new
35 culture.

Fact-Finding Exercise

Read the passage again. Read the following statements. Check whether they are True or False. If a statement is false, rewrite the statement so that it is true. Then go back to the passage and find the line that supports your answer.

1. _____ True _____ False   On the first day of class, the professor arrived late, but the students were on time.

   _____

2. _____ True _____ False   The professor decided to study the behavior of Brazilian and American students.

   _____

3. _____ True _____ False   In an American university, it is important to be on time.

   _____

4. _____ True _____ False   In a Brazilian class, the students leave immediately after the class is finished.

_____

5. _____ True _____ False   In an American university, many students probably leave immediately after the class is finished.

_____

6. _____ True _____ False   Most North Americans think a person who is late is disrespectful.

_____

7. _____ True _____ False   In Brazil, most successful people are expected to be on time.

_____

8. _____ True _____ False   As a result of the study, the professor changed the Brazilian students' behavior.

_____

Reach each question carefully. Either circle the letter of the correct answer, or write your answer in the space provided.

1. What is the main idea of the passage?
   a. It is important to be on time for class in the United States.
   b. People learn the importance of time when they are children.
   c. The importance of being on time differs among cultures.

2. Why did the professor study the Brazilian students' behavior?
   a. The students seemed very rude to him.
   b. He wanted to understand why the students came late.
   c. He wanted to make the students come to class on time.

3. a. Read lines 1 and 2. What does **punctual** mean?

   _____

   b. How do you know?

   _____

4. In line 8, what does **few** refer to?
   a. The professor
   b. The students
   c. Greetings

5. Read lines 7 and 8.

    a. What does **as** mean?

       1. Because

       2. When

       3. If

    b. What is **rude behavior?**

       1. Impolite behavior

       2. Noisy behavior

       3. Studious behavior

6. a. Read lines 10–12. Which is an example of an informal situation?

      _____

    b. Which is an example of a formal situation?

      _____

    c. How do you know?

      _____

    d. What does this word mean?

       1. The same as

       2. In the same order

       3. Opposite

7. Read lines 13–15. How does **on the other hand** connect the American idea of lateness with the Brazilian idea of lateness?

    a. It shows a similarity.

    b. It gives more information.

    c. It shows a contrast.

8. Read lines 17 and 18: "Neither the teacher nor the students always arrive at the appointed hour." Who arrives at the appointed hour?

    a. No one

    b. The students only

    c. The teacher and the students

9. Read lines 18 and 19: "Classes not only begin at the scheduled time in the United States, but they also end at the scheduled time." What does **not only ... but ... also** mean?

    a. And

    b. But

    c. So

10. In line 26, what does **in fact** indicate?

    a. A contrast between two ideas

    b. Something that is true

    c. Emphasis of the previous idea

11. Read lines 31–33. What does **instead** show?

    a. A similarity

    b. A substitution

    c. An opposite

Read the passage again. Underline what you think are the main ideas. Then scan the reading and complete the following flowchart, using the sentences that you have underlined to help you. You will use this flowchart later to answer questions about the reading.

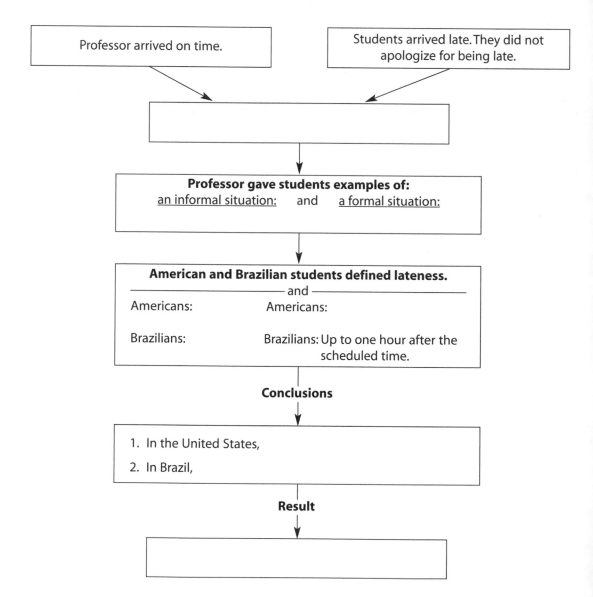

Professor arrived on time.

Students arrived late. They did not apologize for being late.

Professor gave students examples of:
an informal situation: and   a formal situation:

American and Brazilian students defined lateness.
———————————— and ————————————
Americans: Americans:

Brazilians: Brazilians: Up to one hour after the scheduled time.

Conclusions

1. In the United States,

2. In Brazil,

Result

Information Recall and Summary

Read each question carefully. Use your flowchart to answer the questions. Do not refer back to the passage. When you are finished, write a brief summary of the reading.

1. What did the professor decide to study?

   _____

2. Describe the professor's experiment.

   _____

   _____

3. Did American students and Brazilian students have the same ideas about lateness in class? Do classes always begin and end at the appointed hour in both cultures?

   _____

   _____

4. What were the American students' and the Brazilian students' ideas about being late for a lunch appointment?

   _____

   _____

5. In general, what did the Brazilian students think about people who are late?

   _____

6. In general, what did the American students think about people who are late?

_____

7. What was the result of the professor's study?

_____

Summary

Work in pairs or alone. Write a brief summary of the reading, and put it on the blackboard. Compare your summary with your classmates'. Which one best describes the main idea of the reading?

_____

_____

_____

_____

E. Word Forms

PART 1

In English, verbs change to nouns in several ways. Some verbs become nouns by adding the suffix -ing—for example, *feel (v.)* becomes *feeling (n.)*.

Complete each sentence with the correct form of the words on the left. **Use the correct tense of the verb in either the affirmative or the negative form. Use the singular or plural form of the noun.**

spell *(v.)*
spelling *(n.)*

1. a. Allen _____ several words incorrectly on his composition yesterday.
    b. He has to check the _____ of a difficult word before he uses it.

understand *(v.)*
understanding *(n.)*

2. a. Andrew didn't _____ anything in his first math class yesterday.
    b. However, his _____ will improve during the semester.

end *(v.)*
ending *(n.)*

3. a. Please don't tell me the _____ of this mystery story.
    b. I want to guess how the story _____ by myself.

greet *(v.)*
greeting *(n.)*

4. a. "Hi," "Hello," and "How are you" are common _____ in the United States.
    b. Most people _____ each other with a smile.

meet *(v.)*
meeting *(n.)*

5. a. Our department has ten monthly _____ every year.
    b. We _____ during May or December.

PART 2

In English, verbs change to nouns in several ways. Some verbs become nouns by adding the suffix -ation—for example, *combine (v.)* becomes *combination (n.)*.

Complete each sentence with the correct form of the words on the left. **Use the correct tense of the verb in either the affirmative or the negative form. Use the singular or plural form of the noun.**

adapt *(v.)*
adaptation *(n.)*

1. a. Next year a big film company _____ a story from a book to make a movie.

    b. The _____ of a book to a movie takes a lot of work and time.

interpret *(v.)*
interpretation *(n.)*

2. a. Chris is studying at the university for a degree in _____.

    b. When he graduates, he _____ for an embassy.

expect *(v.)*
expectation *(n.)*

3. a. Some people have high _____ when they visit another country.

    b. They want to enjoy themselves. They _____ to have a bad time.

observe *(v.)*
observation *(n.)*

4. a. Suzie is in the park now. She _____ the behavior of pigeons.

    b. She records all her _____ in a special notebook.

explain *(v.)*
explanation *(n.)*

5. a. We needed an _____ of the difference between adjectives and adverbs.

    b. The teacher _____ the difference to us, and we understood.

Vocabulary in Context

adapt *(v.)*	greets *(v.)*	punctual *(adj.)*
apologized *(v.)*	in fact	rude *(adj.)*
appropriate *(adj.)*	prestige *(n.)*	unacceptable *(adj.)*
behavior *(n.)*		

Read the following sentences. Complete each blank space with the correct word or phrase from the list above. Use each word or phrase only once.

1. A suit and tie are _____ clothes for a business meeting.

2. Wearing shorts in a church is _____.

3. In most countries, doctors have considerable _____. People respect them highly.

4. Greg always _____ people by smiling and saying hello.

5. It was very _____ of Martin to ask Mrs. Barnes her age.

6. Being _____ for a job interview is important in order to make a good impression.

7. When you walk into a dark room from the bright sunlight, your eyes need a few moments to _____ to the change in light.

8. It is very cold in Antarctica. _____, it is the coldest place on Earth.

9. Martha dropped chocolate ice cream on my white rug. She _____, but I told her not to worry about it, and we cleaned it up.

10. I don't understand Mark's _____. He gets angry for no reason and refuses to talk to anyone.

G. Topics FOR Discussion AND Writing

1. Describe how people in your culture feel about someone who is late. For example, do you think that person is inconsiderate and irresponsible, or do you think that person is prestigious and successful? Please explain your answer, and also give some examples.

2. How do you think the professor adapted his behavior in Brazil after his study? Why do you think he changed his behavior? Why didn't he try to change the Brazilian students' behavior?

3. **Write in your journal.** Do you think it is important to adapt your behavior to a new culture? In what ways would you be willing to make changes? Please explain.

There are many differences in customs among cultures. In the table below, list some cultural differences between this country and your country, or between your country and another country you have visited. Compare your list with your classmates' lists.

Cultural Difference	_____ (Your Country)	_____ (Other Country)
1. clothes: school work		
2.		
3.		
4.		
5.		

Cloze Quiz

CHAPTER 1: A CULTURAL DIFFERENCE: BEING ON TIME

Read the passage below. Fill in the blanks with one word from the list. Use each word only once.

adapt	difference	greeted	misinterpret	punctual
appointment	ended	hand	neither	rude
behavior	fact	instead	nor	status
contrast	formal	late	only	unacceptable

In the United States, it is important to be on time, or _____ (1), for an appointment, a class, a meeting, etc. However, this may not be true in all countries. An American professor discovered this _____ (2) while teaching a class in a Brazilian university. The two-hour class began at 10 A.M. and _____ (3) at 12 P.M. On the first day, when the professor arrived on time, no one was in the classroom. Many students came after 10 A.M. Several arrived after 10:30 A.M. Two students came after 11 A.M. Although all the students _____ (4) the professor as they arrived, few apologized for their lateness. Were these students being _____ (5)? He decided to study the students' _____ (6).

The professor talked to American and Brazilian students about lateness in both an informal and a _____ (7) situation: lunch with a friend and in a university class. He gave them an example and asked them how they would react. If they had a lunch _____ (8) with a friend, the average American student defined lateness as 19 minutes after the agreed time. On the other _____ (9), the average Brazilian student felt the friend was late after 33 minutes.

In an American university, students are expected to arrive at the appointed hour. In _____ (10), in Brazil, neither the teacher _____ (11) the students always arrive at the appointed hour. Classes not _____ (12) began at the scheduled time in the United States, but they also end at the scheduled time. In the Brazilian class, only a few students left the class at noon; many remained past 12:30 to discuss the class and ask more questions. While arriving late may not be very important in Brazil, _____ (13) is staying late.

The explanation for these differences is complicated. People from Brazilian and North American cultures have different feelings about lateness. In Brazil, the students believe that a person who usually arrives _____ (14) is probably more successful than a person who is always on time. In _____ (15), Brazilians expect a person with _____ (16) or prestige to arrive late, while in the United States lateness is usually disrespectful and _____ (17). Consequently, if a Brazilian is late for an appointment with a North American, the American may _____ (18) the reason for the lateness and become angry.

As a result of his study, the professor learned that the Brazilian students were not being disrespectful to him. _____ (19), they were simply behaving in the appropriate way for a Brazilian student in Brazil. Eventually, the professor was able to _____ (20) his own behavior so that he could feel comfortable in the new culture.

Changing Lifestyles and New Eating Habits

Prereading Preparation

1. What are **lifestyles?** Give examples of two very different lifestyles. Describe how they are different.

2. Think about your life today. Is your life different today than it was three or four years ago? Write about some differences in your life now. List them in the chart below, and tell a classmate about them.

My Life Today	My Life 3 or 4 Years Ago

3. How do you think American lifestyles are changing? Read the title of this article. What do you think this article is about? What examples do you think the author will give?

Changing Lifestyles and New Eating Habits

Americans today have different eating habits than they had in the past. There is a wide selection of food available. They have a broader knowledge of nutrition, so they buy more fresh fruit and vegetables than ever before. At the same time, Americans purchase increasing quantities of sweets, snacks, and sodas.

Statistics show that the way people live determines the way they eat. American lifestyles have changed. They now include growing numbers of people who live alone, single parents and children, and double-income families. These changing lifestyles are responsible for the increasing number of people who must rush meals or sometimes skip them altogether. Many Americans have less time than ever before to spend preparing food. Partly as a consequence of this limited time, 60% of all American homes now have microwave ovens. Moreover, Americans eat out nearly four times a week on the average.

It is easy to study the amounts and kinds of food that people consume. The United States Department of Agriculture (USDA) and the food industry—growers, processors, marketers, and restaurateurs—compile sales statistics and keep accurate records. This information not only tells us what people are eating, but also tells us about the changes in attitudes and tastes. Red meat, which used to be the most popular choice for dinner, is no longer an American favorite. Instead, chicken, turkey, and fish have become more popular. Sales of these foods have greatly increased in recent years. This is probably a result of the awareness of the dangers of eating food that contains high levels of cholesterol, or animal fat. Doctors believe that cholesterol is a threat to human health.

According to a recent survey, Americans also change their eating patterns to meet the needs of different situations. They have certain ideas about which foods will increase their athletic ability, help them lose weight, make them alert for business meetings, or put them in the mood for romance. For example, Americans choose pasta, fruit, and vegetables, which supply them with carbohydrates, to give them strength for physical activity, such as sports. Adults choose foods rich in fiber, such as bread and cereal, for breakfast, and salads for lunch to prepare them for business appointments. For romantic dinners, however, Americans choose shrimp and lobster. While many of these ideas are based on nutritional facts, some are not.

Americans' awareness of nutrition, along with their changing tastes and needs, leads them to consume a wide variety of foods—foods for health, for fun, and simply for good taste.

Fact-Finding Exercise

Read the passage again. Read the following statements. Check whether they
are True or False. If a statement is false, rewrite the statement so that it is true.
Then go back to the passage and find the line that supports your answer.

1. _____ True _____ False   Americans eat the same way they did in the
past.

_____

2. _____ True _____ False   Americans do not eat many sweets anymore.

_____

3. _____ True _____ False   Most Americans do not have a lot of time to
prepare food.

_____

4. _____ True _____ False   Red meat is the most popular American choice for dinner.

_____

5. _____ True _____ False   Americans eat out about four times a week.

_____

6. _____ True _____ False   The USDA keeps information about the food Americans buy.

_____

7. _____ True _____ False   It is healthy to eat food with high cholesterol levels.

_____

8. _____ True _____ False   Americans choose foods rich in fiber for romantic dinners.

_____

Read each question carefully. Either circle the letter of the correct answer, or write your answer in the space provided.

1. What is the main idea of the passage?
   a. American eating habits have changed because of changing lifestyles.
   b. Americans have a greater awareness of nutrition than they did years ago.
   c. Americans have less time than ever before to prepare meals.

2. In line 3–5, what are **quantities?**
   a. Kinds
   b. Amounts
   c. Types

3. Read lines 7–10.
   a. What are **lifestyles?**
      1. The way people live
      2. The way people eat
      3. The way people dress
   b. What is a **double-income family?**
      1. A family that makes twice as much money as another family
      2. A family in which one adult has two jobs
      3. A family in which two adults work full-time

4. Read lines 12 and 13. What does **on the average** mean?
   a. Exactly
   b. Approximately
   c. Sometimes

5. In lines 14–17, what are examples of jobs in the food industry?
   _____

6. Read lines 18–20. What is **red meat?**
   a. Chicken
   b. Fish
   c. Beef

7. a. In line 21–23, what is **cholesterol?**

   _____

   b. How do you know?

   _____

8. In lines 31 and 32, what does **however** indicate?
   a. An explanation
   b. A similarity
   c. A contrast

9. Read lines 32 and 33.
   a. What does **while** mean?
      1. During
      2. Although
      3. Also
   b. What does **some** refer to?
      1. Ideas
      2. Facts
      3. Americans

10. In line 34, what does **along with** mean?
    a. Except for
    b. Together with
    c. Instead of

Read the passage again. Underline what you think are the main ideas. Then scan the reading and complete the following flowchart, using the sentences that you have underlined to help you. You will use this flowchart later to answer questions about the reading.

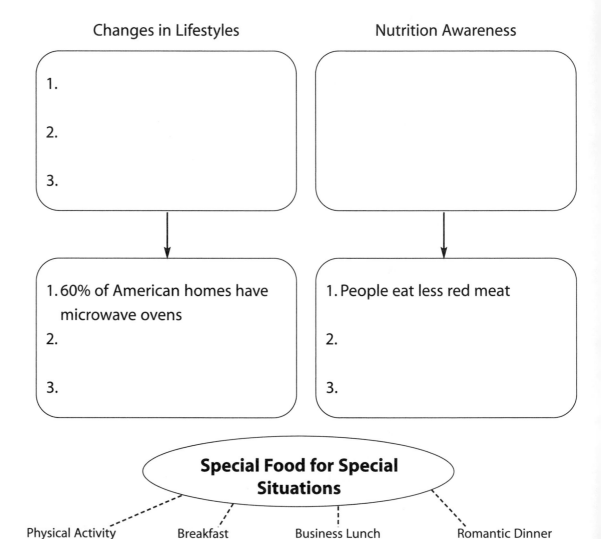

Changes in Lifestyles

1.

2.

3.

Nutrition Awareness

60% of American homes have microwave ovens

1. 60% of American homes have microwave ovens

2.

3.

1. People eat less red meat

2.

3.

Special Food for Special Situations

Physical Activity

Breakfast

Business Lunch

Romantic Dinner

Information Recall and Summary

Read each question carefully. Use your flowchart to answer the questions. Do not refer back to the passage. When you are finished, write a brief summary of the reading.

1. Why do Americans have different eating habits today?

   _____

   _____

2. a. How have American lifestyles changed? Give examples.

   _____

   _____

   b. How do these changing lifestyles affect the way they eat?

   _____

   _____

3. What have Americans learned about cholesterol in food?

   _____

4. How has the awareness of the danger of cholesterol changed what people eat?

   _____

   _____

5. How do people change their eating patterns according to different situations? Give examples.

   _____

   _____

Summary

Work in pairs or alone. Write a brief summary of the reading, and put it on the blackboard. Compare your summary with your classmates'. Which one best describes the main idea of the reading?

_____

_____

_____

_____

_____

E. Word Forms

PART 1

In English, verbs change to nouns in several ways. Some verbs become nouns that represent people by adding the suffix -er—for example, *teach (v.)* becomes *teacher (n.)*.

Complete each sentence with the correct form of the words on the left. **Use the correct tense of the verb in either the affirmative or the negative form. Use the singular or plural form of the noun.**

grow *(v.)*
grower *(n.)*

1. a. Thomas _____ flowers in his garden. He only plants vegetables.
   b. He is an expert, so other _____ in his neighborhood often ask him for advice.

market *(v.)*
marketer *(n.)*

2. a. The various _____ of fruit must ship their produce in refrigerated trucks.
   b. They _____ a new type of apple next season.

consume *(v.)*
consumer *(n.)*

3. a. Enthusiastic _____ of fruit are very demanding. They want only the freshest fruit.
   b. They _____ tons of fruit every year.

employ *(v.)*
employer *(n.)*

4. a. When she began her own company, Ms. Harris _____ anyone who had very little experience.
   b. Like other _____, she wanted experienced people who didn't need much training.

work *(v.)*
worker *(n.)*

5. a. Mark is a very dependable _____.
   b. He always _____ hard and does his job well.

In English, adjectives can change to verbs. Some adjectives become verbs by adding the suffix -en—for example, *light (adj.)* becomes *lighten (v.)*.

Complete each sentence with the correct form of the words on the left. **Use the correct tense of the verb in either the affirmative or the negative form.**

broad *(adj.)*
broaden *(v.)*

1. a. Betty went to college to study French, but she felt that her major was not _____ enough.
    b. Next semester she _____ her major to Romance languages, and study Spanish and Portuguese as well as French.

wide *(adj.)*
widen *(v.)*

2. a. The government _____ the old highway, although it is too narrow.
    b. Instead, the government is planning a new highway, which will be very _____.

sweet *(adj.)*
sweeten *(v.)*

3. a. Joseph loves to drink very _____ coffee.
    b. He _____ his coffee by adding four teaspoons of sugar to his cup.

short *(adj.)*
shorten *(v.)*

4. a. The factory workers want a _____ work week, so they had a demonstration at the factory.
    b. The company _____ their work week to only 4 days a week next month.

long *(adj.)*
lengthen *(v.)*

5. a. The American government _____ some weekends because midweek holidays are inconvenient.
    b. Now some holidays are celebrated on Monday, so everyone has a _____ weekend.

Vocabulary in Context

alert *(adj.)*	habit *(n.)*	skip *(v.)*
awareness *(n.)*	nutritional *(adj.)*	survey *(n.)*
compile *(v.)*	rush *(v.)*	variety *(n.)*
favorite *(adj.)*		

Read the following sentences. Complete each blank space with the correct word from the list above. Use each word only once.

1. Children like a _____ of food in their diet. For example, at breakfast they like to choose among cereal, pancakes, doughnuts, or eggs and toast.

2. If you do not understand one part of the test, you can _____ to the next part and go back to the difficult part later.

3. Joan's train was scheduled to leave at 6 P.M. It was 5:50, so she had to _____ in order not to miss her train.

4. Dean and Jenny are going to _____ a list of all the places they want to visit on their next trip across the country.

5. I like all kinds of cake, cookies, and ice cream, but my _____ dessert is chocolate ice cream. I like it best of all!

6. The college cafeteria manager is going to do a _____ of the students to help her decide which foods students prefer.

7. Small children have very little _____ of the dangers of running into the street.

8. Fruit and vegetables are an important part of a _____ diet.

9. Many students drink large quantities of coffee to keep them _____ while they are studying for an important exam.

10. Ann has a _____ of smoking cigarettes with her morning coffee.

G. Topics FOR *Discussion* AND *Writing*

1. Are lifestyles also changing in your country? Why? Describe how they are changing. Are they similar to the lifestyles in the United States today?

2. In your country, do people eat differently today than they did in the past? Give reasons and examples in your explanation.

3. In your country, what do you eat in various situations (for example, to increase athletic ability, to lose weight, to be alert for business, for romance)? Why?

4. **Write in your journal.** Describe your present lifestyle. What do you like about it? What do you dislike about it?

Non - Traditional American Households

Millions of Households

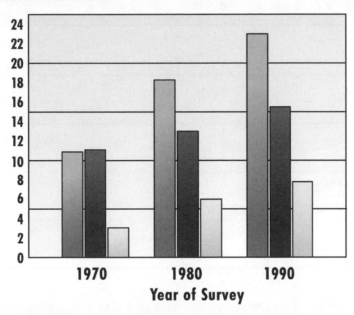

One person   Dual Income   Single parent

1. Refer to the bar graph. Read the following sentences, and fill in the blank spaces with the correct answer.

   a. There were _____ million one-person households in the United States in 1970.

   b. There were _____ million dual-income households in the United States in 1980.

   c. There were _____ million single-parent households in the United States in 1990.

   d. From 1970 to 1990, the greatest increase was in _____ households.

   e. From 1980 to 1990, the smallest increase was in _____ households.

2. Many different factors can affect the way we eat. For example, if you are a very busy person, you may not have a lot of time for meals. As a result, you may not cook very much or you may eat out often. On the other hand, you may have a lot of free time. How would this affect your eating habits? Think about some different factors, list them below, and write about how they affect eating habits.

Factor	Effect on Eating Habits
1. time	
2. money	
3.	
4.	
5.	

CHAPTER 2: CHANGING LIFESTYLES AND NEW EATING HABITS

Read the passage below. Fill in the blanks with one word from the list. Use each word only once.

alert	compile	favorite	nearly	skip
along	consequence	habits	nutrition	survey
average	consume	however	quantities	threat
awareness	example	lifestyles	recent	variety

Americans today have different eating _____ than in the past. There is a
(1)
wide selection of food available. They have a broader knowledge of _____, so
(2)
they buy more fresh fruit and vegetables than ever before. At the same time, Americans
purchase increasing _____ of sweets, snacks, and sodas.
(3)

Statistics show that the way people live determines the way they eat. American
_____ have changed. They now include growing numbers of people who live
(4)
alone, single parents and children, and double-income families. These changing lifestyles
are responsible for the increasing number of people who must rush meals or sometimes
_____ them altogether. Many Americans have less time than ever before to
(5)
spend preparing food. Partly as a _____ of this limited time, 60% of all
(6)
American homes now have microwave ovens. Moreover, Americans eat out
_____ four times a week on the _____.
(7)   (8)

It is easy to study the amounts and kinds of food that people _____. The
(9)
United States Department of Agriculture (USDA) and the food industry—growers, processors, marketers, and restaurateurs—_____ sales statistics and keep accurate
(10)
records. This information not only tells us what people are eating, but also tells us about the

changes in attitudes and tastes. Red meat, which used to be the most popular choice for dinner, is no longer an American _____. Instead, chicken, turkey, and fish have

(11)

become more popular. Sales of these foods have greatly increased in _____

(12)

years. This is probably a result of the _____ of the dangers of eating food that

(13)

contains high levels of cholesterol, or animal fat. Doctors believe that cholesterol is a

_____ to human health.

(14)

According to a recent _____, Americans also change their eating patterns

(15)

to meet the needs of different situations. They have certain ideas about which foods will

increase their athletic ability, help them lose weight, make them _____ for

(16)

business meetings, or put them in the mood for romance. For _____,

(17)

Americans choose pasta, fruit, and vegetables, which supply them with carbohydrates, to

give them strength for physical activity, such as sports. Adults choose foods rich in fiber,

such as bread and cereal, for breakfast, and salads for lunch to prepare them for business

appointments. For romantic dinners,_____, Americans choose shrimp and lob-

(18)

ster. While many of these ideas are based on nutritional facts, some are not.

Americans' awareness of nutrition, _____ with their changing tastes and

(19)

needs, leads them to consume a wide _____ of foods—foods for health, for

(20)

fun, and simply for good taste.

Dreams: Making Them Work for Us

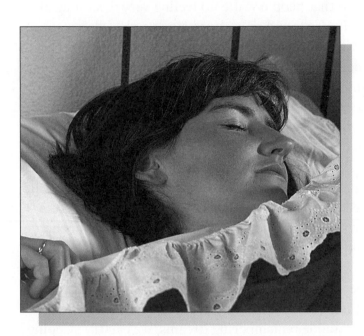

Prereading Preparation

1. What are dreams?

2. How often do you have dreams? Do you usually remember them?

3. Do you think dreams are important? Why or why not? Read the title of this article. What do you think it means?

4. Describe a dream you have had. Then work together with a classmate. Read about each other's dream. What do you think your classmate's dream means?

My Dream

_____

_____

_____

_____

5. Have you ever had a nightmare (a bad dream)? How did you feel after you woke up?

Dreams: Making Them Work for Us

Several nights a week Joseph woke up screaming from the same terrible dream. Joseph could never recall his whole dream, though. He only remembered that someone was running after him. Joseph was trying to get away, but in his dream he could not move. He continued having this nightmare for months. He was so tired in the morning that it was hard for him to go to work. Joseph, you see, is not a frightened child, but a grown man.

Milton Kramer is a psychiatrist and dream researcher in Cincinnati, Ohio. He believes that it is very important that people don't ignore their dreams, because they are messages from our sleeping minds. When Kramer studied dreams and dreamers, he found that people wake up feeling very discouraged after they have a bad dream. He also found that after having a good dream, people feel more optimistic. Clearly, dreams can have harmful or beneficial effects. As a result, Kramer believes that we need to learn how to change our bad dreams. When we understand what happened in our dreams, we can change negative, hurtful dreams to positive, helpful ones.

Before we can begin to change a nightmare, however, we first have to remember what happened in our dream. Researchers say there are many ways to do this. We can keep a journal or diary of what we do when we are awake. Then, before going to sleep, we can review our day. This practice helps us connect our dreams with daily life. As we begin to fall asleep, we should remind ourselves that we want to remember our dreams. This reminder helps us to stay in charge. When we wake up, we should lie still while we try to remember our dream. Dream researchers say that by staying in the same sleeping position, we are more likely to recall the dream. We should also try to remember an important word or picture from the dream. This image makes the rest of the dream easier to remember. Finally, if we have trouble remembering dreams, we can try sleeping later. The longer we sleep, the longer and more complex our dreams will be.

Dr. Rosalind Cartwright is a dream researcher, too. She has developed another dream therapy for changing dreams. According to Dr. Cartwright, dream therapy involves four simple steps you can learn on you own. The first step is to recognize when you are having a bad dream that will make you feel helpless or upset the next morning. The second step is to identify what it is about the dream that makes you feel bad—for example, weak instead of strong, or out of control instead of in control. Next, stop any bad dream. You do not have to continue your bad dream, because you are in charge. The last step is to change the negative part of the dream. Sometimes you may have to wake yourself up and change the dream before you return to sleep. Other times it is possible to change the dream while you are still asleep.

39   By using dream therapy, Joseph was able to change his nightmares.
40 Gradually, his bad dreams stopped altogether. He began having more positive
41 dreams and woke up feeling refreshed and cheerful. A night of good dreaming
42 can leave us all in a better mood in the morning. We feel well rested and more
43 optimistic. Stopping a nightmare and changing it to a positive dream experience
44 can be physically and psychologically beneficial to us all.

A. Fact-Finding Exercise

Read the passage again. Read the following statements. Check whether they are True or False. If a statement is false, rewrite the statement so that it is true. Then go back to the passage and find the line that supports your answer.

1. ____ True ____ False   Joseph had the same bad dream for a long time.

   _____

2. ____ True ____ False   Milton Kramer does not believe that dreams are important.

   _____

3. ____ True ____ False   Many people feel discouraged after they have a good dream.

   _____

4. ____ True ____ False   There are many ways to help us remember our dreams.

   _____

5. ____ True ____ False   Our dreams are usually shorter when we sleep a long time.

   _____

6. ____ True ____ False   Dream therapy can help us change our bad dreams.

   _____

7. ____ True ____ False   Joseph's bad dreams never stopped.

   _____

B. Reading Analysis

Read each question carefully. Either circle the letter of the correct answer, or write your answer in the space provided.

1. What is the main idea of the passage?
   a. Joseph was finally able to change his nightmares by using dream therapy.
   b. Dreams are very important, and it is possible to change a bad dream into a good dream.
   c. Dream therapy has four simple steps for success.

2. Read lines 2 and 3. In these two sentences, which word is a synonym for **recall?**

   _____

3. In line 6, what is a **grown man?**
   a. An adult
   b. A frightened child
   c. A tall man

4. Read lines 9–13.
   a. What are **dreamers?**
      1. People who wake up after a dream
      2. People who dream
      3. People who study dreams
   b. In these lines, what is the opposite (antonym) of **discouraged?**
      1. Harmful
      2. Beneficial
      3. Optimistic
   c. What does **harmful** mean?
      1. Dangerous
      2. Discouraged
      3. Optimistic

d.   In these lines, what is the opposite (antonym) of **harmful?**

   1.   Discouraged

   2.   Effects

   3.   Beneficial

5.   Read lines 16–20.

   a.   What does **this** refer to?

   1.   To change a nightmare

   2.   To remember our dreams

   3.   To keep a diary

   b.   What is a **journal?**

   1.   A dream

   2.   A diary

   3.   A review

   c.   What is **this practice?**

   1.   Going to sleep

   2.   Remembering our dreams

   3.   Keeping a journal

6.   Read lines 24–26. What is **this image?**

   a.   An important word or picture

   b.   The whole dream

   c.   The way we sleep

7.   Read lines 29 and 30. "**According to** Dr. Cartwright" means

   a.   Dr. Cartwright said

   b.   Dr. Cartwright proved

   c.   Dr. Cartwright agreed

8.   Read lines 28–38. Put the following dream therapy steps in the correct order.

   _____ Change the negative part of the dream.

   _____ Identify the part of the dream that makes you feel bad.

   _____ Recognize when you are having a bad dream.

   _____ Stop your bad dream.

9. Read lines 34–41.

   a. **Gradually** means

      1. quickly

      2. slowly

      3. carefully

   b. **Altogether** means

      1. completely

      2. suddenly

      3. gradually

C. Information Organization

Read the passage again. Underline what you think are the main ideas. Then scan the reading and complete the following chart, using the sentences that you have underlined to help you. You will use this chart later to answer questions about the reading.

How to Remember and Change Dreams	
Ways to Remember a Dream	**How to Change a Dream: —Dream Therapy—**
1. During the day: a. b. c. As you fall asleep:	1.
2. When you wake up: a. b.	2. When you wake up: a. b.
3. If you have trouble remembering your dreams:	3. To stop any bad dream:
	4. Change the negative part of the dream: a. b.

Information Recall and Summary

Read each question carefully. Use your chart to answer the questions. Do not refer back to the passage. When you are finished, write a brief summary of the reading.

1. How can we help ourselves remember a dream *before* we go to sleep?

   _____

   _____

   _____

2. How can we help ourselves remember a dream after we wake up?

   _____

   _____

   _____

3. What can we do if we can't remember our dreams?

   _____

   _____

4. Describe the four steps in dream therapy.

   _____

   _____

   _____

   _____

   _____

Summary

Work in pairs or alone. Write a brief summary of the reading, and put it on the blackboard. Compare your summary with your classmates'. Which one best describes the main idea of the reading?

_____

_____

_____

_____

PART 1

In English, verbs change to adjectives in several ways. Some verbs become adjectives by adding the suffix *-ful*—for example, *doubt (v.)* becomes *doubtful (adj.)*.

Complete each sentence with the correct form of the words on the left. **Use the correct tense of the verb in either the affirmative or the negative form.**

cheer *(v.)*
cheerful *(adj.)*

1. a. When Rachel was in the hospital, her friends visited her and _____ her up.
   b. She felt very _____ after their visits.

help *(v.)*
helpful *(adj.)*

2. a. Curt had a headache, so he took some aspirin, but they _____. His headache didn't go away.
   b. Because the aspirin weren't _____, Curt had to leave work early.

rest *(v.)*
restful *(adj.)*

3. a. Next month, Henry is going on vacation. He _____ for two weeks.
   b. His job is quite stressful, so he needs a _____ vacation this year.

use *(v.)*
useful *(adj.)*

4. a. Maureen always _____ a typewriter to do her schoolwork when she was in high school. She didn't like computers.
   b. When she entered college, she learned how to use a computer and realized just how _____ it really was.

harm *(v.)*
harmful *(adj.)*

5. a. Most people know that cigarettes are very _____ to a smoker's health.
   b. However, cigarette smoke can also _____ the health of people who live with smokers.

In English, some adjectives have two forms, depending on their meaning. Some adjectives have an *-ed* form and an *-ing* form—for example, *excited* and *exciting*.

Complete each sentence with the correct adjective form of the words on the left.

frightened *(adj.)*
frightening *(adj.)*

1. a. Craig saw a very _____ movie last Saturday.
    b. He was so _____ that his friends walked home with him.

tired *(adj.)*
tiring *(adj.)*

2. a. Standing all day at work is a _____ experience.
    b. Many people become _____ just from standing on a hard floor.

discouraged *(adj.)*
discouraging *(adj.)*

3. a. The teacher gave his students a very difficult math test. The results of the test were very _____ because none of the students did well.
    b. The teacher was very _____, but he reviewed the math with the class and gave another test. This time the students' grades were much better.

refreshed *(adj.)*
refreshing *(adj.)*

4. a. During the summer, Gloria swims in her pool every afternoon because it's so _____.
    b. She always feels cool and _____ after her afternoon swim.

interested *(adj.)*
interesting *(adj.)*

5. a. The class is quite _____ in going to the Natural History Museum.
    b. The museum has an extremely _____ exhibit on tropical rain forests that the students want to see.

Vocabulary in Context

Read the following sentences. Complete each blank space with the correct word from the list above. Use each word only once.

altogether (adv.)	gradually (adv.)	journal (n.)
cheerful (adj.)	grown (adj.)	practice (n.)
discouraged (adj.)	harmful (adj.)	recall (v.)
dream (v.)		

1. I have met Trudy's brother several times, but I can't _____ his name.

2. Janet keeps her _____ on her computer. She has written in it regularly for several years.

3. Olga wanted to improve her typing speed, so she practiced every day. _____ she became a skilled typist.

4. Simon is a very _____ person. He always seems happy and optimistic.

5. The teacher has a useful _____ of writing our homework on the blackboard every day.

6. After a busy day, I almost always _____ when I go to bed at night.

7. Many children are afraid of the dark, but by the time they are _____, they have overcome their fear.

8. William wanted to stop drinking coffee, so every week he drank fewer cups. For one week, he drank five cups a day. Then he drank four cups a day for another week. After four weeks, he was able to stop drinking coffee _____.

9. Over a long period of time, not getting enough sleep may be _____ to your health.

10. Jason feels _____ about learning Russian. He studied for his Russian test, but he still didn't do well.

G. Topics FOR *Discussion* AND *Writing*

1. Read the last paragraph of the article again. Write about Joseph's nightmares. How do you think he changed them?

2. In many cultures, certain themes in dreams have specific meanings. For example, in the United States, a dream about falling usually means that we feel helpless or out of control. Flying generally means that we feel successful and satisfied with ourselves. Being chased in a dream often signifies a danger from other people. In your culture, do falling, flying, and being chased have the same meaning, or different ones? Think about how your culture interprets dreams. Discuss this and give examples.

3. **Write in your journal.** Describe a dream that you had. What do you think it means?

Follow-Up Activity

Refer back to the chart in Exercise C. Review the four steps in changing a dream. Use the chart below, and begin with the first step: Briefly describe a bad dream that you recently had. Work with a partner. Together, read about each other's dream. Then discuss the other three steps, and help each other identify the negative parts of your dreams and develop strategies for stopping a bad dream and for changing a bad dream. Compare your strategies with your classmates'.

How to Change a Dream: —Dream Therapy—	
Describe a recent bad dream.	
Identify what it was about the dream that made you feel bad.	
Strategies for stopping a bad dream.	
Strategies for changing the negative part of the dream.	

Cloze Quiz

CHAPTER 3: DREAMS: MAKING THEM WORK FOR US

Read the passage below. Fill in the blanks with one word from the list. Use each word only once.

altogether	continued	hard	positive	therapy
changing	dream	identify	recall	tired
charge	gradually	negative	simple	upset
cheerful	grown	next	step	woke

Several nights a week Joseph _____ up screaming from the same terrible
                                    (1)
_____. Joseph could never _____ his whole dream, though. He
      (2)   (3)
only remembered that someone was running after him. He _____ having this
                                                                (4)
nightmare for months. He was so _____ in the morning that it was
                                        (5)
_____ for him to go to work. Joseph, you see, is not a frightened child, but a
      (6)
_____ man.
      (7)

Dr. Rosalind Cartwright has developed a dream therapy for _____ dreams.
                                                                    (8)
According to Dr. Cartwright, dream therapy involves four _____ steps you can
                                                                (9)
learn on your own. The first _____ is to recognize when you are having a bad
                                    (10)
dream that makes you feel helpless or _____ the next morning. The second
                                            (11)
step is to _____ what it is about the dream that makes you feel bad.
              (12)
_____, stop any bad dream. You do not have to continue your bad dream,
      (13)
because you are in _____. The last step is to change the _____
                          (14)   (15)
part of the dream.

By using dream _____, Joseph was able to change his nightmares.
(16)
_____, his bad dreams stopped _____. He began having more
(17)   (18)
_____ dreams and woke up feeling refreshed and _____. A night
(19)   (20)
of good dreaming can leave us all in a better mood in the morning.

J. **Crossword Puzzle**

Clues

Across

4. Happy; in a good mood
6. I usually _____ my coffee with two teaspoons of sugar.
8. An adult is a _____ person.
11. Slowly; little by little
14. Impolite
16. Diary
17. The opposite of *down*
20. Amount
22. It is a bad idea to _____ breakfast. You should eat breakfast every morning.
24. Bad dream
26. John gave me this job. He is my _____.
28. Actions
30. If I hurt someone's feelings, I always _____. I always say that I am sorry.

Down

1. Completely
2. Remember
3. _____, two, three
5. Hurtful; detrimental
7. Picture
9. Although
10. However
12. John feels very _____. He keeps trying to learn English, but he hasn't been successful.
13. People in a new country need to _____, or change, to the different customs.

Down *(continued)*

15. A good _____ reads labels and buys products carefully.

18. Status; rank

19. Way of living

21. Alert

23. I wanted to go to the movies, but I stayed home and studied _____.

25. Farmers _____ wheat, corn, rice, and other grains.

27. We _____ learning English.

29. I come _____ class on time every day.

1. The three chapters in this unit discuss trends in living in the American culture: being on time, changing lifestyles, eating habits, and dreams. Work in a group of three or four and discuss the following questions.

   a. How do these features describe American culture as a whole? What do you think is important to Americans?

   b. Select one of these aspects of American life, and compare it with your own or another culture. How is it similar? How is it different?

2. Think about these features (being on time, changing lifestyles, eating habits, and dreams) of your own culture. Do people in your country feel the same about these features as Americans do? What would you say is important to the people in your culture?

1. Are Americans today aware of the importance of healthy eating habits? Are they willing to give up their favorite foods to improve their nutrition? Why or why not?

2. Watch the video once or twice. Then read below and answer whether the following statements are true (T) or false (F).

    ____ T ____ F 1. According to a survey, 8 out of 10 Americans are aware that good nutrition is moderately or very important.

    ____ T ____ F 2. Most people think that a variety of food is necessary for a balanced diet.

    ____ T ____ F 3. Healthy people should consume fat for more than 30% of their calories.

    ____ T ____ F 4. About 39% of Americans don't want to give up their favorite foods.

    ____ T ____ F 5. It's okay to have our favorite snacks sometimes if we also modify our diets by having low fat milk, leaner meat, and other healthier foods.

3. What habits in many American lifestyles make it hard for people to maintain healthy diets? List a few habits or trends in lifestyles that make people obese.

Surfing THE INTERNET

Use a search engine such as Netscape, Yahoo, Google, or Excite to look up information available from the USDA. Type in "USDA Food Pyramid Guide" and read about the food groups there. How many servings a day should you have from each group? Is the answer different for men, women, or children? Print out a copy of the food pyramid for yourself.

Optional Activity: What other information can you discover about your favorite foods? Enter a famous brand name of one of your favorite foods and search the web site of the product for nutritional information. Is the food you enjoy healthy? Does the web site have any information about how to eat a healthy diet?

UNIT 2

ISSUES IN SOCIETY

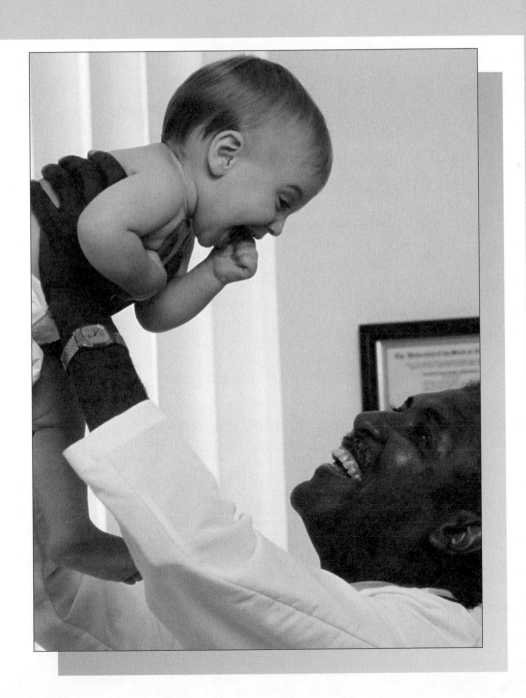

4

Language: Is It Always Spoken?

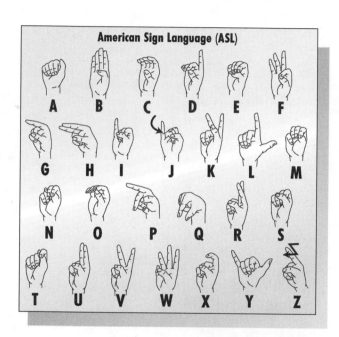

American Sign Language (ASL)

Prereading Preparation

1. What is language?

   a. Work with two partners and write a definition of the word **language** in the box below.

   b. Write your group's definition of **language** on the blackboard. Compare your definition with your classmates' definitions.

   c. Look up the word **language** in your dictionary, and compare it to your definition.

Your Group's Definition	The Dictionary Definition

2. At what age do most babies learn to speak? How do they learn to speak?

3. How do you think deaf babies learn to communicate?

4. How do deaf people communicate?

5. Look at the American Manual Alphabet. Who uses it and why?

   a. In groups of three, use the sign language chart to learn to "sign" an object in the room—for example, **chair** or **pen.**

   b. Demonstrate your word to your classmates, and they will give the name of the object.

6. Read the title of this passage. Reread your definitions of **language.** Do you think human language must be spoken? Is there any other way that people can communicate?

Language: Is It Always Spoken?

1　　　Most of us know a little about how babies learn to talk. From the time
2　infants are born, they hear language because their parents talk to them all the
3　time. Between the ages of seven and ten months, most infants begin to make
4　sounds. They repeat the same sounds over and over again. For example, a baby
5　may repeat the sound "dadada" or "bababa." This activity is called babbling.
6　When babies babble, they are practicing their language. Soon, the sound
7　"dadada" may become "daddy," and "bababa" may become "bottle."
8　　　What happens, though, to children who cannot hear? How do deaf children
9　learn to communicate? Recently, doctors have learned that deaf babies babble
10　with their hands. Laura Ann Petitto, a psychologist at McGill University in
11　Montreal, Canada, has studied how children learn language. She observed three
12　hearing infants and two deaf infants. The three hearing infants had English-
13　speaking parents. The two deaf infants had deaf mothers and fathers who used
14　American Sign Language (ASL) to communicate with each other and with their
15　babies. Dr. Petitto studied the babies three times: at 10, 12, and 14 months.
16　During this time, children really begin to develop their language skills.
17　　　After watching and videotaping the children for several hundred hours, the
18　psychologist and her assistants made many important observations. For
19　example, they saw that the hearing children made many different, varied
20　motions with their hands. However, there appeared to be no pattern to these
21　motions. The deaf babies also made many different movements with their hands,
22　but these movements were more consistent and deliberate. The deaf babies
23　seemed to make the same hand movements over and over again. During the four-
24　month period, the deaf babies' hand motions started to resemble some of the
25　basic hand-shapes used in ASL. The children also seemed to prefer certain
26　hand-shapes.
27　　　Hearing infants start first with simple syllable babbling (dadada), then put
28　more syllables together to sound like real sentences and questions. Apparently,

29 deaf babies follow this same pattern, too. First, they repeat simple hand-shapes.
30 Next, they form some simple hand signs (words) and use these movements
31 together to resemble ASL sentences.

32   Linguists—people who study language—believe that our ability for lan-
33 guage is innate. In other words, humans are born with the capacity for language.
34 It does not matter if we are physically able to speak or not. Language can be
35 expressed in many different ways—for instance, by speech or by sign. Dr. Petitto
36 believes this theory and wants to prove it. She plans to study hearing children
37 who have one deaf parent and one hearing parent. Dr. Petitto wants to see what
38 happens when babies have the opportunity to learn both sign language and
39 speech. Does the human brain prefer speech? Some of these studies of hearing
40 babies who have one deaf parent and one hearing parent show that the babies
41 babble equally with their hands and their voices. They also produce their first
42 words, both spoken and signed, at about the same time.

43   The capacity for language is uniquely human. More studies in the future
44 may prove that the sign system of the deaf is the physical equivalent of speech. If
45 so, the old theory that only the spoken word is language will have to be changed.
46 The whole concept of human communication will have a very new and different
47 meaning.

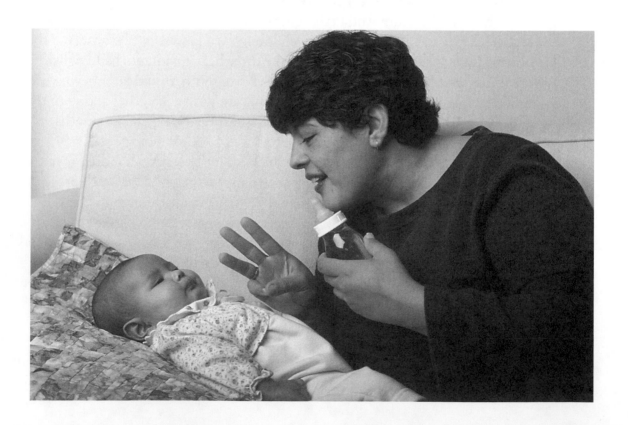

Fact-Finding Exercise

Read the passage again. Read the following statements. Check whether they are True or False. If a statement is false, rewrite the statement so that it is true. Then go back to the passage and find the line that supports your answer.

1. _____ True _____ False   Most infants start to babble before they are a year old.

_____

2. _____ True _____ False   Dr. Petitto studied only deaf babies.

_____

3. _____ True _____ False   The psychologist saw that deaf babies and hearing babies moved their hands the same way.

_____

4. _____ True _____ False   Dr. Petitto believes that we are all born with the ability for language.

_____

5. _____ True _____ False   Dr. Petitto believes that hearing babies who have one deaf parent and one hearing parent produce their first spoken words before their first signed words.

_____

Reach each question carefully. Either circle the letter of the correct answer, or write your answer in the space provided.

1. What is the main idea of the passage?

    a. Both deaf children and hearing children learn to communicate in similar ways at about the same time.

    b. Children begin to develop their language skills at around two years of age.

    c. Many linguists believe that all humans are born with the ability to speak.

2. Read lines 3–7. What is **babbling?**

    _____

3. Read lines 13–15.

    a. What is **ASL?**

    _____

    b. Who uses ASL? Why?

    _____

4. Read lines 17–20. What is an **observation?**

    a. Something you see or hear

    b. Something you write

    c. Something important

5. In lines 18–21, what are **varied motions?**

    a. Different sounds

    b. Different movements

    c. Different signs

6. Read lines 19–23: "...they saw that the hearing children made many different, varied motions with their hands. However, there appeared to be no pattern to these motions. The deaf babies also made many different movements with their hands, but these movements were more consistent and deliberate. The deaf babies seemed to make the same hand movements over and over again."

    a. Which of the following statements are true?

        1. All children make motions with their hands.

        2. Only the deaf children made many different movements with their hands.

        3. The hearing children's hand movements had a pattern.

        4. The deaf children's hand movements had a pattern.

    b. Complete the following sentence correctly.
        Both the deaf and the hearing children made movements with their hands, but

        1. only the hearing children made different movements

        2. they all made the same movements over and over again

        3. only the deaf children repeated the same hand motions

        4. only the hearing children repeated the same hand motions

7. Read lines 23–25: "During the four-month period, the deaf babies' hand motions started to resemble some of the basic hand-shapes used in ASL." This sentence means that

    a. the deaf babies were studying ASL

    b. the deaf babies were repeating their parents' hand signs

    c. the deaf babies stopped babbling

8. Read lines 32 and 33: "Linguists—people who study language—believe that our ability for language is innate. In other words, humans are born with the capacity for language."

    a. What is a **linguist?**

        _____

    b. How do you know?

        _____

    c. What does **capacity** mean?

       1. Language

       2. Ability

       3. Belief

    d. What does **innate** mean?

       1. Something you are born with

       2. Something you are able to do

       3. Something a linguist believes

    e. What follows **in other words?**

       1. A new idea

       2. An explanation of the previous idea

       3. An example of the previous idea

9. a. In lines 34–36, what are some different ways we can express language?

    _____

    b. What does **for instance** mean?

       1. However

       2. So that

       3. For example

10. Read lines 43–45.

    If so means

    a. if everyone agrees

    b. if this is true

Information Organization

Read the passage again. Underline what you think are the main ideas. Then scan the reading and complete the following outline, using the sentences that you have underlined to help you. You will use this outline later to answer questions about the reading.

I. How Babies Learn Language

    A. Hearing Babies

        1.

        2.

    B.

        1.

        2.

II.

    A. Who Conducted the Experiment:

    B. Who She Studied:

    C. How She Studied Them:

    D. Conclusion:

III. Future Experiments

    A. Theory:

    B. Who She Will Study:

    C. Purpose of the Experiment:

Information Recall and Summary

Read each question carefully. Use your outline to answer the questions. Do not refer back to the passage. When you are finished, write a brief summary of the reading.

1. a. What is babbling?

   _____

   b. When does it occur?

   _____

2. Who did Dr. Petitto study? Why?

   _____

3. What did the psychologist and her assistants discover after they watched the videotapes of the children?

   _____

4. What theory does Dr. Petitto believe about language learning?

   _____

5. Who does this psychologist want to study next? Why?

   _____

Summary

Work in pairs or alone. Write a brief summary of the reading, and put it on the blackboard. Compare your summary with your classmates'. Which one best describes the main idea of the reading?

_____

_____

_____

_____

Word Forms

PART 1

In English, verbs change to nouns in several ways. Some verbs become nouns by adding the suffix -ing—for example, *learn (v.)* becomes *learning (n.)*.

Complete each sentence with the correct form of the words on the left. **Use the correct tense of the verb in either the affirmative or the negative form. Use the singular or plural form of the noun.**

talk *(v.)*
talking *(n.)*

1. a. For most people, _____ is an important social activity.
   b. Unfortunately, some people _____ too much.

begin *(v.)*
beginning *(n.)*

2. a. Harry needs to rewrite his composition. He _____ each paragraph with an indentation, but he should have.
   b. A composition needs an indentation at the _____ of every paragraph.

hear *(v.)*
hearing *(n.)*

3. a. The school nurse checks the _____ of all the students in every class.
   b. If a child _____ well, the nurse informs the parents and suggests that they take their child to a doctor.

babble *(v.)*
babbling *(n.)*

4. a. Rod and Cheryl's baby _____ all the time.
   b. They are very excited about her _____ because she is saying "mamma" and "dada."

mean *(v.)*
meaning *(n.)*

5. a. The verb *get* _____ so many different things that I sometimes have trouble understanding it in a sentence.
   b. The word *get* has so many different _____ that I become confused.

PART 2

In English, adjectives change to nouns in several ways. Some adjectives become nouns by changing the final -t to -ce—for example, *ignorant (adj.)* becomes *ignorance (n.)*.

Complete each sentence with the correct form of the words on the left. **Use the singular or plural form of the noun.**

important *(adj.)*
importance *(n.)*

1. a. Whether you write a composition with a pen or pencil is of very little _____.
   b. What is much more _____ is the content of the composition.

different *(adj.)*
difference *(n.)*

2. a. Some languages aren't very _____ from each other, for example, Spanish and Portuguese.
   b. Other languages, however, have significant _____, for example, Chinese and French.

significant *(adj.)*
significance *(n.)*

3. a. The introduction of the personal computer several years ago had _____ effects on our everyday lives.
   b. We can understand the unbelievable _____ of this machine when we realize that today there are tens of millions of PCs in the United States alone.

dependent *(adj.)*
dependence *(n.)*

4. a. As children grow up, their _____ on their parents decreases.
   b. However, children usually remain financially _____ on their parents for many years.

persistent *(adj.)*
persistence *(n.)*

5. a. Rebecca is an incredibly _____ person. She studied hard for four years to get a scholarship to college.
   b. As a result of her _____, she did well on her tests and got a scholarship to a good university.

Vocabulary in Context

Read the following sentences. Complete each blank space with the correct word or phrase from the list above. Use each word or phrase only once.

capacity (n.)	in other words	observation (n.)
for instance	meaning (n.)	persistent (adj.)
if so	motion (n.)	varied (adj.)
innate (adj.)		

1. Eugene is a very _____ student. He never stops working until he finishes a job, regardless of how difficult it is for him.

2. It may rain on Saturday. _____, we won't go on a picnic. We'll see a movie instead.

3. If Jackie doesn't understand the _____ of a word from the context, she uses her English dictionary.

4. Animals do not have the _____ for speech. Only humans can communicate with language.

5. Henry has a _____ life. During the day, he is a student. In the evenings, he works as a waiter. On Saturdays, he teaches swimming to children, and on Sundays, he sings in a choir.

6. Researchers have to have training in _____. They need to learn what to look for and how to record what they see.

7. Human babies have many _____ abilities. Walking and speaking are two of them.

8. In different cultures, the same _____, such as waving your hand, may have different meanings.

9. Janet complains about everything. She's always too warm or too cold. She doesn't like anything. _____, Janet is a very negative person.

10. Matthew enjoys going out to restaurants to experience eating the food of different cultures. _____, one month he will go to an Indian restaurant. Then he will try Japanese food. After that, he will go to a Columbian or a Greek restaurant.

G. *Topics* FOR *Discussion* AND *Writing*

1. Many famous people of the past and present have been deaf. Despite their disability, they were successful in their lives. For example, Helen Keller was an important author and scholar, and Marlee Matlin is a famous American actress. What other famous people do you know who were or are hearing-impaired (deaf)? Write about one of these people. Tell about what that person has accomplished in spite of his or her disability.

2. Sign language is one important form of nonverbal communication. Can you think of another type of nonverbal communication? Describe it.

3. **Write in your journal.** Is it important for you to learn sign language? Why or why not?

1. Doctors have developed a controversial operation (a cochlear implant) to enable the deaf to "hear." Many deaf people are opposed to this operation. They say that they are not really disabled. They feel they are a minority group and should be accepted as they are—nonhearing people. They feel it is wrong to force children to have this operation and that the operation does not really enable the deaf to hear as well as nondeaf people do anyway. They feel that their sign language should be accepted as any spoken language is.

   Work in a group of four. Make a list of the advantages and disadvantages of remaining deaf (and not having the operation) and the advantages and disadvantages of having the operation. Next to your list of advantages and disadvantages, write the consequences of remaining deaf and the consequences of being able to "hear." Compare your list with your classmates' lists.

2. Many deaf people feel that ASL is a real language. They believe that hearing people should learn it, just as they learn other languages. The American Manual Alphabet on page 60 is only for spelling out words, letter by letter. Go to the library and find a book on learning ASL. In small groups, learn to "sign" some basic rules and sentences. Then, in your group, discuss what it may be like to learn ASL, compared to learning a spoken language. Discuss your conclusions with your classmates.

CHAPTER **4**   Language: Is It Always Spoken?

Cloze Quiz

CHAPTER 4: LANGUAGE: IS IT ALWAYS SPOKEN?

Read the passage below. Fill in the blanks with one word from the list. Use each word only once.

babies	example	matter	pattern	same
capacity	innate	movements	prefer	speech
consistent	language	observations	psychologist	varied
deaf	learn	over	resemble	words

Recently, doctors have learned that deaf _____ babble with their hands.
(1)
Laura Ann Petitto, a _____ at McGill University in Montreal, Canada, has studied
(2)
how children _____ language. She observed three hearing infants and two
(3)
_____ infants. After watching and videotaping the children for several hundred
(4)
hours, the psychologist and her assistants made many important _____. For
(5)
_____, they saw that the hearing children made many different,
(6)
_____ motions with their hands. However, there appeared to be no
(7)
_____ to these motions. The deaf babies also made many different
(8)
_____ with their hands, but these movements were more _____
(9)   (10)
and deliberate. The deaf babies seemed to make the _____ hand movements
(11)
over and _____ again. During the four-month period, the deaf babies' hand
(12)
motions started to _____ some of the basic hand-shapes used in ASL. The chil-
(13)
dren also seemed to _____ certain hand-shapes.
(14)

Linguists—people who study language—believe that our ability for language is
_____. In other _____, humans are born with the _____
(15)   (16)   (17)
for language. It does not _____ if we are physically able to speak or not.
(18)
_____ can be expressed in many different ways—for instance, by
(19)
_____ or by sign.
(20)

5

Loneliness: How Can We Overcome It?

Prereading Preparation

1. What is **loneliness?**

2. Are **loneliness** and being **alone** the same? Why or why not?

3. Look at the table below. Work with a partner and make a list of some reasons why people may feel lonely. Have you or your partner ever felt lonely for these reasons? Discuss your answers with your classmate.

Reasons People Feel Lonely	You	Your Partner
1.	yes/no	yes/no
2.	yes/no	yes/no
3.	yes/no	yes/no
4.	yes/no	yes/no
5.	yes/no	yes/no

4. Do you think everyone feels lonely at some time in his or her life? Do you think this is common? Explain your answer.

5. How would you answer the question in the title of this chapter?

Loneliness: How Can We Overcome It?

Most people feel lonely sometimes, but it usually only lasts between a few minutes and a few hours. This kind of loneliness is not serious. In fact, it is quite normal. For some people, though, loneliness can last for years. Psychologists are studying this complex phenomenon in an attempt to better understand long-term loneliness. These researchers have already identified three different types of loneliness.

The first kind of loneliness is temporary. This is the most common type. It usually disappears quickly and does not require any special attention. The second kind, situational loneliness, is a natural result of a particular situation—for example, a divorce, the death of a loved one, or moving to a new place. Although this kind of loneliness can cause physical problems, such as headaches and sleeplessness, it usually does not last for more than a year. Situational loneliness is easy to understand and to predict.

The third kind of loneliness is the most severe. Unlike the second type, chronic loneliness usually lasts more than two years and has no specific cause. People who experience habitual loneliness have problems socializing and becoming close to others. Unfortunately, many chronically lonely people think there is little or nothing they can do to improve their condition.

Psychologists agree that one important factor in loneliness is a person's social contacts, e.g., friends, family members, coworkers, etc. We depend on various people for different reasons. For instance, our families give us emotional support, our parents and teachers give us guidance, and our friends share similar interests and activities. However, psychologists have found that the number of social contacts we have is not the only reason for loneliness. It is more important how many social contacts we think or expect we should have. In other words, though lonely people may have many social contacts, they sometimes feel they should have more. They question their own popularity.

Most researchers agree that the loneliest people are between the ages of 18 and 25, so a group of psychologists decided to study a group of college freshmen. They found that more than 50% of the freshmen were situationally lonely at the beginning of the semester as a result of their new circumstances, but had adjusted after a few months. Thirteen percent were still lonely after seven months due to shyness and fear. They felt very uncomfortable meeting new people, even though they understood that their fear was not rational. The

35 situationally lonely freshmen overcame their loneliness by making new friends,
36 but the chronically lonely remained unhappy because they were afraid to do so.
37   Psychologists are trying to find ways to help habitually lonely people for
38 two reasons. First of all, they are unhappy and unable to socialize. Secondly,
39 researchers have found a connection between chronic loneliness and serious
40 illnesses such as heart disease. While temporary and situational loneliness can
41 be a normal, healthy part of life, chronic loneliness can be a very sad, and
42 sometimes dangerous, condition.

Fact-Finding Exercise

Read the passage again. Read the following statements. Check whether they are True or False. If a statement is false, rewrite the statement so that it is true. Then go back to the passage and find the line that supports your answer.

1. _____ True _____ False   Psychologists say there are two different kinds of loneliness.

   _____

2. _____ True _____ False   All kinds of loneliness last only a short time.

   _____

3. _____ True _____ False   Temporary loneliness is very serious.

   _____

4. _____ True _____ False   Divorce sometimes causes loneliness.

   _____

5. _____ True _____ False   Loneliness can cause sleeplessness and headaches.

   _____

6. _____ True _____ False   Chronic loneliness usually lasts more than two years.

   _____

7. _____ True _____ False   Lonely people have no social contacts.

   _____

8. _____ True _____ False   The loneliest people are over 50 years old.

   _____

9. _____ True _____ False   Chronic loneliness can cause serious illness.

   _____

Reading Analysis

Read each question carefully. Either circle the letter of the correct answer, or write your answer in the space provided.

1. What is the main idea of the passage?
   a. There are three kinds of loneliness.
   b. Chronic loneliness is the most severe kind.
   c. Researchers want to cure loneliness.

2. Read lines 1–5.
   a. What does **last** mean?
      1. Finish
      2. Hurt
      3. Continue
   b. What does **this complex phenomenon** refer to?
      1. Loneliness that lasts for years
      2. Loneliness that lasts for hours

3. Read lines 14–17.
   a. What does **unlike** show?
      1. A similarity
      2. A difference
      3. An addition
   b. Which word in these sentences is a synonym for **chronic?**

      _____

4. Read lines 19 and 20.
   a. What follows **e.g.?**
      1. Examples
      2. Proof
      3. Explanations

b. What does **etc.** mean?
      1. For example
      2. And others
      3. End of sentence

5. In line 21, **for instance** introduces
   a. explanations
   b. examples
   c. results

6. Read lines 25–27. How does **in other words** help you?

   _____

   _____

7. In line 27, what does **question** mean?
   a. Ask a question
   b. Have doubts about

8. Read lines 34–36.
   a. What does "the situationally lonely freshmen overcame their loneliness" mean?
      1. They accepted their loneliness.
      2. They were no longer lonely.
      3. They made new friends.
   b. What does …" they were afraid to do so" mean?

      _____

9. Read lines 40–42. What does **while** mean?
   a. At the same time
   b. During
   c. Although

Information Organization

Read the passage again. Underline what you think are the main ideas. Then scan the reading and complete the following flowchart, using the sentences that you have underlined to help you. You will use this flowchart later to answer questions about the reading.

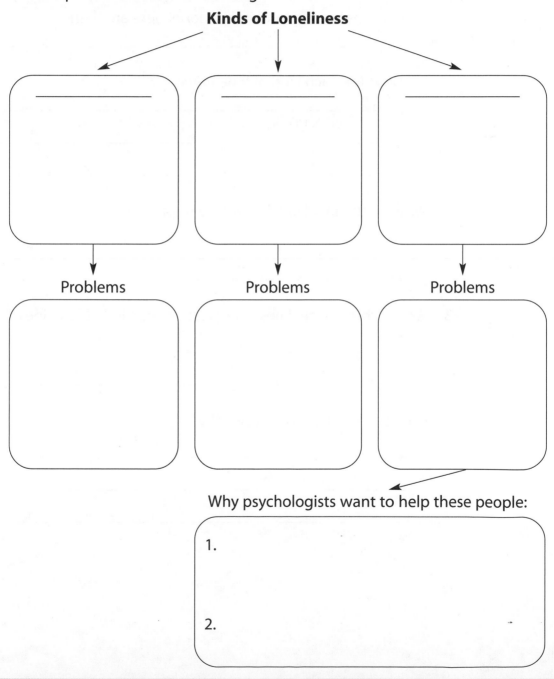

Kinds of Loneliness

Problems
Problems
Problems

Why psychologists want to help these people:

1.

2.

Read each question carefully. Use your flowchart to answer the questions. Do not refer back to the passage. When you are finished, write a brief summary of the reading.

1. a. How many different kinds of loneliness are there?

   _____

   b. Describe each kind of loneliness.

   _____

   _____

   _____

2. Why is situational loneliness easy to predict?

   _____

   _____

3. Why is chronic loneliness the most severe kind of loneliness?

   _____

   _____

4. How can loneliness be unhealthy?

   _____

   _____

   _____

Summary

Work in pairs or alone. Write a brief summary of the reading, and put it on the blackboard. Compare your summary with your classmates'. Which one best describes the main idea of the reading?

_____

_____

_____

_____

Word Forms

PART 1

In English, adjectives become nouns in several ways. Some adjectives become nouns by adding the suffix -ness—for example, *sick (adj.)* becomes *sickness (n.)*. Complete each sentence with the correct form of the words on the left. **Use the singular or plural form of the noun.**

happy *(adj.)*
happiness *(n.)*

1. a. My nieces are very _____ children.
    b. Their _____ is important to my sister.

ill *(adj.)*
illness *(n.)*

2. a. The teacher left school early because she felt _____ during class.
    b. Fortunately, her _____ seemed to improve by the next morning.

lonely *(adj.)*
loneliness *(n.)*

3. a. My aunt overcame her _____ by going out more often with her friends.
    b. She was very _____ after her husband died.

shy *(adj.)*
shyness *(n.)*

4. a. Some doctors think that _____ children are born that way.
    b. This _____ often prevents them from doing well in school.

sleepless *(adj.)*
sleeplessness *(n.)*

5. a. My father finally went to the doctor because his _____ was so severe.
    b. After several _____ nights, he was exhausted.

In English, some adjectives become nouns by adding the suffix *-ity*—for example, *national (adj.)* becomes *nationality (n.)*.

Complete each sentence with the correct form of the words on the left. **Use the singular or plural form of the noun.**

complex *(adj.)*
complexity *(n.)*

1. a. The _____ of math depends on the type of math. For example, arithmetic is very simple.
    b. In contrast, calculus is a very _____ subject.

popular *(adj.)*
popularity *(n.)*

2. a. One of the most _____ fast foods in the United States is the hamburger.
    b. Its incredible _____ will probably continue for many years.

similar *(adj.)*
similarity *(n.)*

3. a. England and the United States are _____ because the people speak the same language.
    b. However, culturally, there are fewer _____ and many differences.

rational *(adj.)*
rationality *(n.)*

4. a. Under ordinary circumstances, most people act in a _____ manner.
    b. Under unusual circumstances, however, many people's level of _____ decreases.

equal *(adj.)*
equality *(n.)*

5. a. The American Constitution guarantees _____ to everyone under the law.
    b. In other words, every person living in the United States has _____ rights.

Vocabulary in Context

chronic (adj.)	predicted (v.)	shy (adj.)
factors (n.)	remain (v.)	temporary (adj.)
for instance	severe (adj.)	unlike (adj.)
overcame (v.)		

Read the following sentences. Complete each blank space with the correct word or phrase from the list above. Use each word or phrase only once.

1. Helen is very thin, _____ her sister, who is quite heavy.

2. After I learn English, I will _____ in this country and get a good job.

3. This beautiful weather is only _____. It is going to rain for the rest of this week.

4. Artie finally _____ his fear of flying when he went to Florida by plane.

5. I am always waiting for Debbie because she is late for everything. Her _____ lateness is destroying our friendship.

6. Yolanda is a _____ student. She is very quiet and always sits alone in class.

7. This morning, the newscaster _____ snow for tomorrow.

8. My uncle went to the hospital because he suddenly had a _____ pain in his back.

9. A proper diet and frequent exercise are important _____ in maintaining good health.

10. Barbara has many varied interests. _____, she enjoys music, horseback riding, and coin collecting.

G. Topics FOR Discussion AND Writing

1. In this article, the author states that young adults (18 to 25 years old) are the loneliest people in the United States. Think about this statement. What do you think may be some reasons for this?

2. Do you think it is important for psychologists and researchers to study loneliness? Why or why not?

3. **Write in your journal.** Describe a time in your life when you felt lonely. What did you do to overcome your loneliness?

H. Follow-Up Activity

In the article, the author states that in the United States, the loneliest people are young adults (18 to 25 years old). Is this also true in your country? Are different people lonely in different cultures? Take a survey in your class. Ask your classmates who the loneliest people are in their cultures. Then put the results of the survey on the blackboard. With your classmates, discuss what you think are the reasons for these results.

Country	Loneliest Age	Possible Reasons
U.S.A.	18–25	Many young people are in college and away from home.

Cloze Quiz

CHAPTER 5: LONELINESS: HOW CAN WE OVERCOME IT?

Read the passage below. Fill in the blanks with one word from the list. Use each word only once.

chronic	habitual	normal	predict	shyness
circumstances	instance	overcame	rational	temporary
connection	interests	phenomenon	remained	unfortunately
factor	loneliness	popularity	severe	words

Most people feel lonely sometimes, but it usually only lasts between a few minutes and a few hours. This kind of loneliness is not serious. In fact, it is quite _____.
(1)
For some people, though, loneliness can last for years. Psychologists are studying this complex _____ in an attempt to better understand long-term loneliness.
(2)
These researchers have already identified three different types of loneliness.

The first kind of loneliness is _____. This is the most common type. It
(3)
usually disappears quickly and does not require any special attention. The second kind, situational _____, is a natural result of a particular situation—for example, a
(4)
divorce, the death of a loved one, or moving to a new place. Although this kind of loneliness can cause physical problems, such as headaches and sleeplessness, it usually does not last for more than a year. Situational loneliness is easy to understand and to

_____.
(5)
The third kind of loneliness is the most _____. Unlike the second type,
(6)
chronic loneliness usually lasts more than two years and has no specific cause. People who experience _____ loneliness have problems socializing and becoming close to
(7)
others. _____, many chronically lonely people think there is little or nothing
(8)
they can do to improve their condition.

Psychologists agree that one important _____ in loneliness is a person's
(9)
social contacts, e.g., friends, family members, coworkers, etc. We depend on various people
for different reasons. For _____, our families give us emotional support, our
(10)
parents and teachers give us guidance, and our friends share similar _____
(11)
and activities. However, psychologists have found that the number of social contacts we
have is not the only reason for loneliness. It is more important how many social contacts we
think or expect we should have. In other _____, though lonely people may
(12)
have many social contacts, they sometimes feel they should have more. They question their
own _____.
(13)

Most researchers agree that the loneliest people are between the ages of 18 and 25, so
a group of psychologists decided to study a group of college freshmen. They found that
more than 50% of the freshmen were situationally lonely at the beginning of the semester
as a result of their new _____, but had adjusted after a few months. Thirteen
(14)
percent were still lonely after seven months due to _____ and fear. They felt
(15)
very uncomfortable meeting new people, even though they understood that their fear was
not _____. The situationally lonely freshmen _____ their loneli-
(16)   (17)
ness by making new friends, but the chronically lonely _____ unhappy
(18)
because they were afraid to do so.

Psychologists are trying to find ways to help habitually lonely people for two reasons.
First of all, they are unhappy and unable to socialize. Secondly, researchers have found a
_____ between chronic loneliness and serious illnesses such as heart disease.
(19)
While temporary and situational loneliness can be a normal, healthy part of life,
_____ loneliness can be a very sad, and sometimes dangerous, condition.
(20)

6

The Importance of Grandmothers

Prereading Preparation

1. Work in a small group. Talk about your grandmothers.

    a. What memories do you have of them from your childhood? For example, what did you do when you were with your grandmothers? How did they treat you? What food or gifts did they give you?

    b. Did both of your grandmothers always treat you the same? In what ways did one grandmother treat you differently from your other grandmother? Use the chart below to write your answers.

	My Father's Mother	My Mother's Mother
How did they treat you the same?		
How did they treat you differently?		

3. As a class, share your information about your grandmothers. Make a list on the blackboard of all the students' responses. What differences are there between your fathers' mothers and your mothers' mothers?

4. Read the title of this passage. What do you think you are going to read about?

The Importance of Grandmothers

1 What do you think of when you think about your grandmothers? Many
2 people have happy memories of their grandmothers. Their grandmothers loved
3 them, paid attention to them, and gave them special treats, such as toys and
4 sweets. Sometimes, grandmothers even helped them when they had problems
5 with their parents. It seems that for many people, their grandmothers were a
6 very happy part of their childhood.
7 In recent years, anthropologists have begun to study the role of
8 grandmothers. Anthropologists are scientists who study people, societies, and
9 cultures. They studied infants and children to learn about the factors that
10 helped infants and children survive. Anthropologists usually looked at parents
11 and did not pay much attention to grandparents. However, now they are
12 studying how grandmothers also influence the survival rate of their
13 grandchildren.
14 Many biologists and anthropologists now believe that the role of
15 grandmothers in a family is very important. Grandmothers may be the reason
16 why human infants, who take so many years to grow up, are able to survive. The
17 biologists and anthropologists are starting to examine grandmothers within
18 different societies and cultures. In fact, at one international conference, the role
19 of grandmothers was the main topic. The biologists and anthropologists
20 explained that although grandmothers no longer have children, many grandmothers
21 are still young and active. As a result, they have the time and energy to help
22 with their grandchildren. This extra help may be an important factor in
23 reducing the mortality, or death, rate among young children.
24 Some people at the conference studied different societies. They explained
25 that in many cultures, having a grandmother in the family made a significant
26 difference in the child's chances of living. In fact, the grandmother's presence
27 sometimes improved a child's chance of survival even more than the father's
28 presence did. In other words, it was sometimes more important for a child to
29 have a grandmother than for a child to have a father!
30 Dr. Ruth Mace and Dr. Rebecca Sear work in the Department of
31 Anthropology at University College in London. They collected and studied
32 information about people in the countryside in Gambia, Africa. At the time of
33 their study, the child mortality rate was very high. Dr. Mace and Dr. Sear looked
34 at children who were about one to three years old. They discovered that the

presence or absence of the child's father did not affect the death rate. However, the presence of a grandmother reduced the children's chances of dying by 50%. These anthropologists made another discovery that surprised them very much. The children were only helped by the presence of their maternal grandmother— their mother's mother. The presence of their father's mother, or paternal grandmother, had no effect on the mortality rate.

Dr. Cheryl Jamison is an anthropologist at Indiana University in Bloomington. She worked with colleagues to study the population records of a village in central Japan for the period 1671 through 1871. They found that the mortality rate for children in the village was very high. In fact, 27.5% of children died by the age of 16. They then studied girl and boy children separately and looked for the presence of grandmothers. Again, the anthropologists were surprised by their discovery. The death rate for girls was not different whether or not a grandmother lived with them. However, there was a great difference in the survival rate of boys. If a maternal grandmother lived in the household, boys were 52% less likely to die in childhood. The anthropologists were very surprised to find that boys were 62% more likely to die in childhood when a paternal grandmother lived in the household. Dr. Jamison said that in this society, families usually lived with the husband's parents, so very few children lived with their maternal grandmothers.

Today, many children do not live with their grandmothers. However, grandmothers still have an important role in their grandchildren's lives. They still love and care for their grandchildren, and make their lives happier, too.

A. Fact-Finding Exercise

Read the passage again. Read the following statements. Check whether they are True or False. If a statement is false, rewrite the statement so that it is true. Then go back to the passage and find the line that supports your answer.

1. ____ True ____ False   Anthropologists believe that grandmothers often help their grandchildren survive.

_____

2. ____ True ____ False   Many grandmothers are too old to help with their grandchildren.

_____

3. ____ True ____ False   Some people at the conference believe that having a grandmother in the family may reduce a child's survival rate.

_____

4. ____ True ____ False   In Gambia, the presence of a father increased a child's survival rate.

_____

5. ____ True ____ False   The death rate for girls in Japan decreased when the grandmother lived with the family.

_____

6. ____ True ____ False   From 1671 to 1871, Japanese families usually lived with the husband's parents.

_____

7. ____ True ____ False   The survival rate for boys in Japan increased when the maternal grandmother lived in the household.

_____

Read each question carefully. Either circle the letter of the correct answer, or write your answer in the space provided.

1. What is the main idea of the passage?

   a. Maternal grandmothers always love their grandchildren more than paternal grandmothers do.

   b. In many cultures, grandmothers play an important role in the lives of their young grandchildren.

   c. Grandfathers play no role at all in the lives of their young grandchildren.

2. Read lines 2–4. What are **treats?**

   a. Toys

   b. Candy

   c. Small gifts

3. Read lines 5 and 6. When is a person's **childhood?**

   a. The period from birth to age 13

   b. The period from birth to age 21

   c. The period from birth to marriage

4. Read lines 7–13.

   a. What is an **anthropologist?**

   _____

   b. What is a **factor?**

      1. A parent or other relative

      2. Something that influences something else

      3. A danger to someone's life

   c. What does **influence** mean?

      1. Assist

      2. Affect

      3. Harm

5. Read lines 15 and 16. What does **survive** mean?

    a. Continue to live

    b. Be happy

    c. Depend on

6. Read lines 22 and 23.

    a. What does **reducing** mean?

        1. Helping

        2. Stopping

        3. Decreasing

    b. What does **mortality** mean?

    _____

    c. How do you know?

    _____

7. Read lines 22 and 23. **This extra help** means

    a. the grandmother's help

    b. the anthropologist's help

    c. the parents' help

8. Read lines 24–26. What does **significant** mean?

    a. Very positive

    b. Very negative

    c. Very important

9. Read lines 38–40.

    a. Which side of a person's family is the **maternal** side?

        1. The father's side

        2. The mother's side

    b. Which side of a person's family is the **paternal** side?

        1. The father's side

        2. The mother's side

c. Your parents' brothers and sisters are your uncles and aunts. Specifically, your mother's brother is

    1. your maternal uncle

    2. your paternal uncle

d. Your father's sister is

    1. your maternal aunt

    2. your paternal aunt

10. Read lines 49–52. A **household** is

    a. the building that a family lives in together

    b. the people who live together in one home

Information Organization

Read the passage a second time. Underline what you think are the main ideas. Then scan the reading and complete the following outline, using the sentences that you have underlined to help you. You will use this outline later to answer questions about the reading.

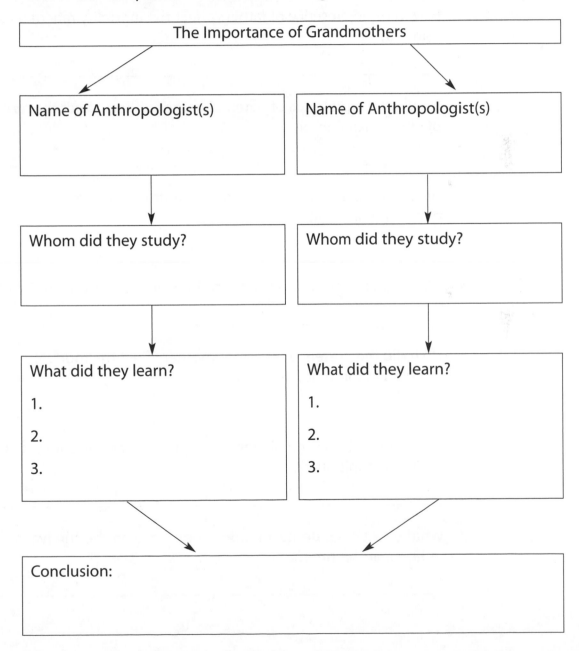

The Importance of Grandmothers

Name of Anthropologist(s)

Name of Anthropologist(s)

Whom did they study?

Whom did they study?

What did they learn?

1.

2.

3.

What did they learn?

1.

2.

3.

Conclusion:

Information Recall and Summary

Read each question carefully. Use your outline to answer the questions. Do not refer back to the passage. When you are finished, write a brief summary of the reading.

1. How did the presence of fathers affect the mortality rate of children in Gambia?

   _____

2. How did the presence of paternal grandmothers affect the mortality rate of children in Gambia?

   _____

3. How did the presence of maternal grandmothers affect the mortality rate of children in Gambia?

   _____

4. What was the mortality rate for children in Japan from 1671 to 1871?

   _____

5. How did the presence of a grandmother affect the mortality rate for girls in Japan at this time?

   _____

6. What effect did maternal grandmothers have on the survival rate of boys in Japan at this time?

   _____

7. What effect did paternal grandmothers have on the survival rate of boys in Japan at this time?

   _____

Summary

Work in pairs or alone. Write a brief summary of the reading, and put it on the blackboard. Compare your summary with your classmates. Which one best describes the main idea of the reading?

_____

_____

_____

_____

_____

E.   Word Forms

PART 1

In English, some verbs become nouns by adding the suffix *-tion*—for example, *collect (v.), collection (n.).*

Complete each sentence with the correct form of the words on the left. **Use the correct tense of the verb in either the affirmative or the negative form. Use the singular or plural form of the noun.**

inform *(v.)*
information *(n.)*

1.   a.   We needed some _____ about the train schedule from New York to Boston.
     b.   We went to the ticket window, and the clerk _____ us that trains leave for Boston every hour.

populate *(v.)*
population *(n.)*

2.   a.   Native Americans first _____ the Western Hemisphere many thousands of years ago. They came in many groups.
     b.   These first Americans spread all over North and South America, and the _____ of all the different groups grew.

examine *(v.)*
examination *(n.)*

3.   a.   Yolanda is having problems with her car. Tomorrow her mechanic _____ it to see what's wrong.
     b.   Yolanda's mechanic uses a computer to help with his _____ of the problems.

explain *(v.)*
explanation *(n.)*

4.   a.   John's three-year-old son asked, "Why is the sky blue?" John had no simple _____ to give him.
     b.   John _____ why the sky is blue. He said, "Ask your mother."

reduce *(v.)*
reduction *(n.)*

5.   a.   Daniel went shopping during a sale. The store _____ the price of a coat he wanted to buy.
     b.   The price _____ was 50 percent! Daniel was very happy.

In English, some adjectives change to nouns by dropping the final -t and adding -ce—for example, *dependent (adj.), dependence (n.).*
Complete each sentence with a correct form of the words on the left.
Use the singular or plural form of the noun.

important *(adj.)* 1. a. Yesterday, the college made an _____
importance (n.) announcement about new exams.
  b. All the students understood the _____ of this announcement.

different *(adj).* 2. a. Although Maria and Sarah are twins, they look
difference *(n.)* _____. They are not identical twins.
  b. There are a few _____ in their appearance. Maria is taller than Sarah and has blue eyes and blonde hair. Sarah has brown eyes and brown hair.

significant *(adj.)* 3. a. Cell phones have had a very _____ effect on
significance *(n.)* people's lives. Today, people can make telephone calls anywhere.
  b. The _____ of this technology and its affect on our everyday lives has been surprising. Now people even talk on the phone while they are driving or eating dinner in a restaurant with friends.

present *(adj.)* 4. a. The entire family's _____ was requested at
presence *(n.)* Catherine's wedding.
  b. Catherine was very happy to have all of her relatives _____ on her wedding day.

absent *(adj.)* 5. a. It snowed very hard last night. As a result, many students
absence *(n.)* were _____ from school.
  b. Because of the number of _____, the teacher cancelled the class.

Vocabulary in Context

absent *(adj.)*	mortality *(n.)*	significant *(adj.)*
factor *(n.)*	present *(adj.)*	survive *(v.)*
household *(n.)*	reduce *(v.)*	treat *(n.)*
influence *(v.)*		

Read the sentences below. Complete each blank space with the correct word from the list above. Use each word only once.

1. Our teacher enjoys holidays. The day before a holiday, she brings in a _____ for every student, and we read about the holiday.

2. The law requires people to wear seat belts in cars. This law has helped to _____ the number of injuries and deaths from car accidents.

3. The _____ rate from car accidents has also decreased as a result of other improvements to cars, such as better brakes.

4. Every 10 years, the U.S. government counts the number of people who live in the United States. The government gets information on every _____, such as family income.

5. An important _____ that helps children survive is the availability of clean water and healthy food.

6. Jane moved to another state last year. One of the most _____ changes in her life was adapting to the difference in weather. Florida is very different from Maine!

7. Our friends often _____ the decisions we make, for example, the type of clothes we wear.

8. Susan was _____ from class yesterday, so she called Ana to ask about the homework.

9. The Mayor had a serious announcement to make, so all the reporters from the city's newspapers were _____ at the Mayor's meeting.

10. When their house caught fire, the family was able to _____ by climbing out a window on the second floor and jumping to the ground. No one was seriously hurt.

G. Topics FOR *Discussion* AND *Writing*

1. In your culture, do grandparents often live with a married child? If so, do they live with a son or a daughter? Think about how grandmothers interact with their sons' children and with their daughters' children. Do they treat the children the same or differently? Explain your answer.

2. In different cultures, the survival rate of children differs, depending on whether the maternal grandmother is present. Children's survival rate does not improve when the paternal grandmother is present. What may be some explanations for this difference? In other words, what do paternal grandmothers and maternal grandmothers do that is different?

3. In our modern world, is it still important for grandparents to live in the same household with their grandchildren? Explain your reasons for your answer.

4. **Write in your journal.** Imagine that you have married children and that they have children. Will you treat your sons' children and your daughters' children the same? Why or why not?

1. Dr. Harald A. Euler is a professor of psychology at the University of Kassell in Germany. He interviewed people about their grandparents. Seven hundred people said that all four of their grandparents were alive until they, the grandchildren, were at least seven years old. Examine the pie chart below. Complete the sentences that follow.

Favorite Grandparent

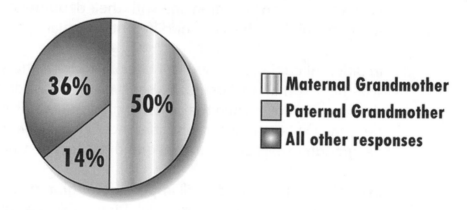

Maternal Grandmother
Paternal Grandmother
All other responses

a. Among the Germans who were interviewed, their favorite grandparent was their _____.

b. Their second favorite was their _____.

c. Thirty-six percent of the Germans gave different responses. What do you think the other responses were? Read the list below and check the responses you think different people gave.

_____ My paternal grandfather was my favorite grandparent.

_____ My maternal grandfather was my favorite grandparent.

_____ All of my grandparents died when I was a baby.

_____ I liked all of my grandparents the same. I do not have a favorite.

_____ My grandparents liked me the best of all their grandchildren.

_____ I did not like any of my grandparents.

2. Dr. Donna Leonetti and Dr. Dilip C. Nath are anthropologists at the University of Washington. They studied two groups of people who live in northeast India today. These groups are Bengali and Khasi, and they have some cultural similarities. For example, the Bengali and the Khasi both have low incomes and do heavy manual labor.

There is one big difference between these cultures. When Bengali couples marry, they live with the husband's parents. When Khasi couples marry, they live with the wife's parents. As a result, Bengali children grow up with their paternal grandparents, and Khasi children grow up with their maternal grandparents.

Examine the bar graph below. Answer the questions that follow.

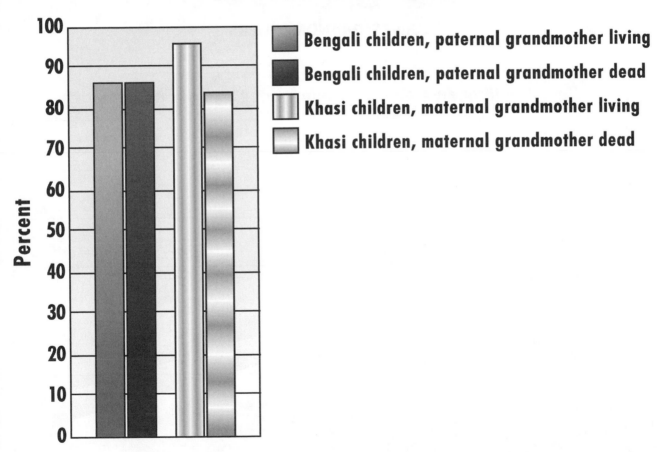

Children Who Survive to Age Six

■ Bengali children, paternal grandmother living
■ Bengali children, paternal grandmother dead
▥ Khasi children, maternal grandmother living
▥ Khasi children, maternal grandmother dead

a. For the Bengali children, did it make a difference in their survival rate to have their paternal grandmother living? _____ Yes _____ No

b. For the Khasi children, did it make a difference in their survival rate to have their maternal grandmother living? _____ Yes _____ No

c. What conclusion can we make from the information about the Bengali and Khasi grandmothers?

   1. Paternal grandmothers and maternal grandmothers treat their grandchildren the same.

   2. Paternal grandmothers and maternal grandmothers treat their grandchildren differently.

3. Refer to the questionnaire below. Go out alone or in pairs. Survey two or three people. Then bring back your data and combine it with the other students' information. How do these results compare with the answers you discussed in your class? Can you make any general statements about the results of your survey? Do people from the same country have similar memories of their grandmothers?

SURVEY: GRANDMOTHERS

	Informant #1	Informant #2	Informant #3
Gender			
Nationality			
Age			
Think about your grandparents. 1. Which grandparent was your favorite?			
2. Did this grandparent live with you and your parents?			
3. Why was this grandparent your favorite?			

Cloze Quiz

CHAPTER 6: THE IMPORTANCE OF GRANDMOTHERS

Read the passage below. Fill in the blanks with one word from the list. Use each word only once.

absence	examine	influence	population	significant
anthropologists	factors	maternal	presence	survival
childhood	grandmothers	memories	reduced	treats
discovery	household	mortality	role	whether

What do you think of when you think about your grandmothers? Many people have happy _____ of their grandmothers. Their grandmothers loved them, paid
(1)

attention to them, and gave them special _____, such as toys and sweets. It
(2)

seems that for many people, their grandmothers were a very happy part of their

_____.
(3)

In recent years, anthropologists have begun to study the role of grandmothers.

_____ are scientists who study people, societies, and cultures. They studied
(4)

infants and children to learn about the _____ that helped infants and children
(5)

survive. Now they are studying how grandmothers _____ the survival rate of
(6)

their grandchildren.

Biologists and anthropologists are starting to _____ grandmothers
(7)

within different societies and cultures. In fact, at one international conference, the

_____ of grandmothers was the main topic. Some people at the conference
(8)

studied different societies. They explained that in many cultures, having a grandmother in

the family made a _____ difference in the child's chances of living. In fact, the
(9)

grandmother's presence sometimes improved a child's chance of _____ even
(10)

more than the father's _____ did. In other words, it was sometimes more
(11)
important for a child to have a grandmother than for a child to have a father!

Dr. Ruth Mace and Dr. Rebecca Sear collected and studied information about people in
Gambia, Africa. They discovered that the presence or _____ of the child's
(12)
father did not affect the death rate. However, the presence of a grandmother
_____ the children's chances of dying by 50%. The children were only helped
(13)
by the presence of their _____ grandmother—their mother's mother. The
(14)
presence of their father's mother, or paternal grandmother, had no effect on the
_____ rate.
(15)

Dr. Cheryl Jamison is an anthropologist at Indiana University in Bloomington. She
studied the _____ records of a village in central Japan for the period 1671
(16)
through 1871. They studied girl and boy children separately and looked for the presence of
_____. Again, the anthropologists were surprised by their _____.
(17)   (18)
The death rate for girls was not different _____ or not a grandmother lived
(19)
with them. However, there was a great difference in the survival rate of boys. If a maternal
grandmother lived in the _____, boys were 52% less likely to die in childhood.
(20)

Unit 2 Review

J.   Crossword Puzzle

Read the clues on the next page. Write the answers in the correct spaces in the puzzle.

Crossword Puzzle Clues

Across

2. The _____ rate refers to the death rate.
5. Ability
8. Susan is unique. She is _____ anyone I have ever met.
9. John is very _____. He has many friends.
10. My father's parents are my _____ grandparents.
11. The past tense of **do**
13. Habitual
15. Very young children _____ before they can make real words.
16. **He, _____, it**
17. Not permanent; only for a time
18. Different
22. An _____ is a person who studies people, cultures, and societies.
23. I live in _____ United States.

Down

1. Sophisticated; not simple
3. A _____ is a person who studies languages.
4. Mary watched her baby carefully to make an _____ about his development.
6. Affect
7. Inborn
9. Some children call their father Daddy; other children call their father _____.
12. Apples are my _____ fruit. I like apples better than any other fruit.
14. My mother's parents are my _____ grandparents.
16. Some people are able to _____ under very difficult conditions.
19. He has; I _____.
20. As children _____ up, their language develops.
21. Man, woman, _____, girl

1. The three topics in this unit discuss different issues in society. How do you think language skills, loneliness, and the role of grandmothers are related? How do they affect each other?

2. Many children live in an extended family, that is, they live with their parents and with grandparents, and perhaps other relatives, too. Do you think their language development is influenced by the presence of more adults? Explain your reasons for your answers.

3. Do people who live in extended families experience less loneliness than people who live in a nuclear family, i.e., a family with parents and children? Explain your reasons for your answers.

1. When parents are absent, can grandparents do a good job raising children? Why or why not?

2. Watch the video once or twice. Then answer the following questions.

   a. Who lives in the Strassburger household?

   _____

   b. Was it a difficult decision for the Strassburgers to accept the role of parents?

   _____

   c. How does the support group help the grandparents who bring up children?

   _____

   d. The Strassburgers are much older than average parents of young children. Do you think age is a significant factor for a parent? Why?

   _____

   e. Do you think the boys will have a happy childhood with their grandparents? Why or why not?

   _____

3. The video does not explain why the Strassburgers are bringing up their grandsons. Name some reasons why grandparents take over parental roles.

Surfing THE INTERNET

Search the Internet for "American Sign Language." When you find a good site, look up useful words to learn in sign language. Look for verbs such as come or go, nouns such as money or book, and adjectives such as *happy* or *sad*. Teach the words to a partner or small group.

Optional Activity: Read more about teaching sign language to young babies. Enter the words "sign language" and "babies" into a search engine. What information can you find? Does everyone support teaching sign language to babies? What are the arguments on the Internet for and against teaching sign language to babies?

UNIT 3

JUSTICE AND CRIME

EQUAL JUSTICE UNDER LAW

Innocent Until Proven Guilty:
The Criminal Court System

Prereading Preparation

1. In groups of three or four, discuss the job of the police. What do you think their responsibilities should be? What should they have the authority to do?

2. Read the title of this chapter. In the American legal system, a person accused of a crime is considered to be innocent until he or she is proven guilty in a court. In your country, does an accused person have to prove his or her innocence, or does the court have to prove the person's guilt?

3. Refer to the photo on page 113. The woman represents justice. Why is she blindfolded? What do the scales in her left hand symbolize? What does the sword in her right hand symbolize?

1   The purpose of the American court system is to protect the rights of the
2 people. According to American law, if someone is accused of a crime, he or she is
3 considered innocent until the court proves that the person is guilty. In other
4 words, it is the responsibility of the court to prove that a person is guilty. It is
5 not the responsibility of the person to prove that he or she is innocent.

6   In order to arrest a person, the police have to be reasonably sure that a
7 crime has been committed. The police must give the suspect the reasons why
8 they are arresting him and tell him his rights under the law.[1] Then the police
9 take the suspect to the police station to "book" him. "Booking" means that the
10 name of the person and the charges against him are formally listed at the police
11 station.

12   The next step is for the suspect to go before a judge. The judge decides
13 whether the suspect should be kept in jail or released. If the suspect has no
14 previous criminal record and the judge feels that he will return to court rather
15 than run away—for example, because he owns a house and has a family—he can
16 go free. Otherwise, the suspect must put up bail.[2] At this time, too, the judge
17 will appoint a court lawyer to defend the suspect if he can't afford one.

18   The suspect returns to court a week or two later. A lawyer from the district
19 attorney's office presents a case against the suspect. This is called a hearing. The
20 attorney may present evidence as well as witnesses. The judge at the hearing
21 then decides whether there is enough reason to hold a trial. If the judge decides
22 that there is sufficient evidence to call for a trial, he or she sets a date for the
23 suspect to appear in court to formally plead guilty or not guilty.

24   At the trial, a jury of 12 people listens to the evidence from both attorneys
25 and hears the testimony of the witnesses. Then the jury goes into a private room
26 to consider the evidence and decide whether the defendant is guilty of the crime.
27 If the jury decides that the defendant is innocent, he goes free. However, if he is
28 convicted, the judge sets a date for the defendant to appear in court again for
29 sentencing. At this time, the judge tells the convicted person what his punishment
30 will be. The judge may sentence him to prison, order him to pay a fine, or place
31 him on probation.[3]

32   The American justice system is very complex and sometimes operates
33 slowly. However, every step is designed to protect the rights of the people. These
34 individual rights are the basis, or foundation, of the American government.

---

[1]The police must say, "You have the right to remain silent. Anything you say can and will be used against you in a court of law. You have the right to speak to a lawyer and to have the lawyer present during questioning. If you so desire, and cannot afford one, a lawyer will be appointed without any charge before any questioning. Do you understand these rights as I have explained them to you?" These rights are called the Miranda rights.

[2]Bail is an amount of money that the accused person pays to the court to assure that he will return to the court on the trial date. If the person comes back, the money is returned to him. If not, the court keeps the bail money.

[3]Probation means that the convicted person does not have to go to jail. Instead, he must follow certain rules and he is supervised by a parole officer.

Fact-Finding Exercise

Read the passage again. Read the following statements. Check whether they are True or False. If a statement is false, rewrite the statement so that it is true. Then go back to the passage and find the line that supports your answer.

1. ____ True ____ False   According to American law, the court must prove that a suspect is innocent.

_____

2. ____ True ____ False   The police decide if a suspect stays in jail or can be released.

_____

3. ____ True ____ False   The judge appoints a court lawyer for a suspect who cannot pay for one.

_____

4. ____ True ____ False   An attorney can present evidence or witnesses at the hearing.

_____

5. ____ True ____ False   There are 12 people on a jury.

_____

6. ____ True ____ False   At a trial, the judge decides if the suspect is guilty or innocent.

_____

7. ____ True ____ False   The jury gives the convicted person his punishment after the trial.

_____

Read each question carefully. Either circle the letter of the correct answer, or write your answer in the space provided.

1. What is the main idea of the passage?
   a. According to the American court system, a suspect must prove that she or he is innocent.
   b. The American court system is very complex and was designed to protect the rights of the people.
   c. According to the American court system, a judge decides if a suspect is innocent or guilty.

2. Read lines 2 and 3: "…he or she is considered innocent …." This means
   a. the law thinks the suspect is innocent
   b. the law must prove the suspect is innocent

3. Read lines 3 and 4. What follows **in other words?**
   a. An example of the previous sentence
   b. A restatement of the previous sentence
   c. A new idea about the court system

4. Read lines 6 and 7. **Reasonably sure** means
   a. very sure
   b. not sure
   c. a little sure

5. a. Read lines 7 and 8: "The police … tell him his rights under the law." What are these rights called?

   _____

   b. How do you know?

   _____

c. This information is called a

1. direction

2. footnote

3. preface

6. Read lines 8–11.

a. In line 9, what does **"booking"** mean?

_____

b. Why does this word have quotation marks (**" "**) around it?

1. It is a new word.

2. Someone is saying this word in the reading.

3. It is a special meaning of the word *book* that the police use.

7. Read lines 12–17.

a. **He can go free** means

1. the suspect is not guilty

2. the suspect does not have to go to trial because the judge has decided he is innocent

3. the suspect does not have to wait in jail or pay money until he goes to trial

b. **Otherwise** means

1. if not

2. in addition

3. in contrast

c. Read the footnote describing **bail.** What is the purpose of having the suspect pay bail?

1. To pay for the judge and the trial

2. As insurance that the suspect will return to court

3. To pay for a court lawyer to defend the suspect

8. Read lines 18 and 19. What is a **hearing?**

_____

9. Read lines 19–23. What is a synonym for **enough reason?**

_____

10. In line 27, **however** means

    a. also

    b. next

    c. but

11. Read lines 27–31.

    a. What is **sentencing?**

        1. Subjects, verbs, and objects

        2. The date the defendant must appear in court

        3. The punishment that the judge gives the defendant

    b. Read the footnote about **probation.** What is the purpose of probation?

        1. To make sure the convicted person behaves well

        2. To save the court some money

12. a. Read lines 33 and 34. What is a synonym for **basis?**

      _____

    b. How do you know?

      _____

      _____

Read the passage again. Underline what you think are the main ideas. Then scan the reading and complete the following flowchart, using the sentences that you have underlined to help you. You will use this flowchart later to answer questions about the reading.

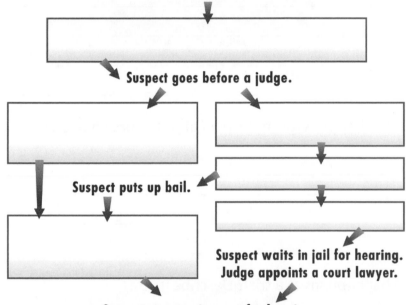

The American Justice System

Police arrest suspect and read Miranda rights.

Suspect goes before a judge.

Suspect puts up bail.

Suspect waits in jail for hearing.
Judge appoints a court lawyer.

Suspect appears in court for hearing.
District Attorney presents case against suspect.

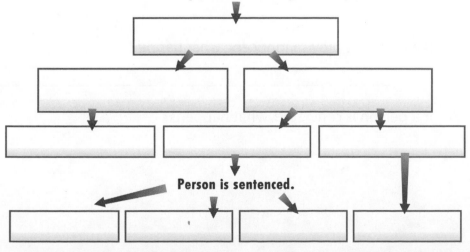

Person is sentenced.

Information Recall and Summary

Read each question carefully. Use your flowchart to answer the questions. Do not refer back to the passage. When you are finished, write a brief summary of the reading.

1. What must the police do after they arrest a suspect?

   _____

   _____

   _____

   _____

   _____

2. What happens to the suspect after the police book him or her?

   _____

   _____

   _____

   _____

3. What happens at a trial? Describe it.

   _____

   _____

4. If a person is proven innocent, what happens?

   _____

5. If a person is convicted, what happens?

   _____

Summary

Work in pairs or alone. Write a brief summary of the reading, and put it on the blackboard. Compare your summary with your classmates'. Which one best describes the main idea of the reading?

_____

_____

_____

_____

_____

PART 1

In English, verbs become nouns in several ways. Some verbs become nouns by adding the suffix *-ment*—for example, *govern (v.)* becomes *government (n.).*

Complete each sentence with the correct form of the words on the left. **Use the correct tense of the verb in either the affirmative or the negative form. Use the singular or plural form of the noun.**

appoint *(v.)*
appointment *(n.)*

1. a. In a few weeks, the President _____ a new ambassador to Japan.
    b. This is a very important _____ because Japan is an economically powerful country.

punish *(v.)*
punishment *(n.)*

2. a. In the American court system, a judge tries to make the _____ fit the crime.
    b. For instance, a judge _____ a convicted person with life in prison for stealing a bicycle.

establish *(v.)*
establishment *(n.)*

3. a. In the United States, the permanent _____ of a democratic government took several years.
    b. The United States _____ a constitutional government in 1787.

disagree *(v.)*
disagreement *(n.)*

4. a. Allison and Clark had several _____ about redecorating their home.
    b. In fact, they _____ on almost everything: paint color, furniture, carpets, and lights.

judge *(v.)*
judgment *(n.)*

5. a. A person who _____ a trial must be impartial when making decisions.
    b. In a court of law, _____ must be made fairly and objectively.

In English, some adjectives become nouns by adding the suffix *-ity*—for example, *national (adj.)* becomes *nationality (n.)*.

Complete each sentence with the correct form of the words on the left. **Use the singular or the plural form of the noun.**

responsible *(adj.)*
responsibility *(n.)*

1. a. Employees have many _____ to their employers.
    b. Employees are usually _____ for coming to work on time, for being productive at work, and for being honest with their employer.

formal *(adj.)*
formality *(n.)*

2. a. On very _____ occasions, especially when they go out, Americans like to dress up.
    b. However, at home, Americans do not observe the same _____. For example, men usually do not wear a suit to go to a friend's house for dinner.

complex *(adj.)*
complexity *(n.)*

3. a. Today, a car is quite a _____ machine. New cars have computers and electronic fuel systems.
    b. In the past, however, cars were much simpler. _____ in machinery developed over many years as technology advanced.

individual *(adj.)*
individuality *(n.)*

4. a. In general, people value their _____.
    b. Even when they are part of a group, people enjoy making _____ decisions.

public *(adj.)*
publicity *(n.)*

5. a. The mayor made a very unpopular _____ announcement yesterday.
    b. He received considerable negative _____ when he announced that he planned to reduce many city services.

F. DICTIONARY SKILLS

Read the following sentences. Use the context to help you understand the boldface words. Read the dictionary entry for that word and circle the appropriate definition. Then rewrite the sentence, using the definition you have chosen. Be sure to make your sentence grammatically correct.

1. The police list the **charges** against a suspect in a book at the police station.

> **charge** /tʃɑrdʒ/ *n.* **1** [C] price. **2** [C] a purchase made on credit. **3** [C] a fast move forward, surge. **4** [C] a statement of blame against s.o.: *a charge against s.o. in a court of law.*

_____

_____

2. The police may not have any **record** of criminal activity for a particular suspect.

> **record** /ˈrɛkərd/ *n.* **1** s.t. (usu. written) that proves that an event happened, including records of business transactions, scientific data, cultural or other human activities. **2** the best time, distance, etc., in an athletic event. **3** a criminal's history of arrests and things he or she did wrong. **4** a flat, black disk onto which a sound recording, esp. music, has been pressed.

_____

_____

3. The judge's first **step** is to decide whether to keep the suspect in jail or to allow him to go free until the hearing.

> **step** /stɛp/ *n.* **1** a walking movement, the act of lifting the foot, moving it forward, and putting it down. **2** the distance of this movement. **3** one surface in a set of stairs. **4** *n. pl.* **steps:** a set of stairs, staircase. **5** one action toward a goal.

_____

_____

4. The district attorney's office **presents** evidence against a suspect.

> **present** /prɪˈzɛnt/ *v.* **1** to offer, put forth for consideration. **2** to give. **3** to bring to meet s.o., esp. of greater importance. **4** to perform: *to present a play.*

_____

_____

5. The jury goes into a private room in order to **consider** the evidence against the suspect and decide whether the suspect is innocent or guilty.

> **consider** /kənˈsɪdər/ *v.* **1** [I;T] to think about s.t.. **2** [T] to debate. **3** [T] to have an opinion about s.t.

_____

_____

Vocabulary in Context

Read the following sentences. Complete each blank space with the correct word or phrase from the list above. Use each word only once.

appoint *(v.)*	establish *(v.)*	present *(v.)*
basis *(n.)*	however *(adv.)*	purpose *(n.)*
case *(n.)*	otherwise *(adv.)*	record *(n.)*
consider *(v.)*		

1. The Board of Health keeps an accurate _____ of all births and deaths in the city.

2. Holly worked very hard before she was able to _____ her own business, but eventually, she was successful.

3. If it snows this week, we will go skiing this weekend. _____ we will stay in the city and see a movie.

4. The students always _____ a class representative for the student council at the beginning of the semester.

5. Every fall, television stations _____ new programs to their viewers.

6. When deciding on a college, you need to _____ several factors, including the cost of tuition, the courses offered, and the location of the college.

7. The ability to read and write well is the _____ of a good education.

8. I don't understand the _____ of this machine. What is it used for?

9. I prefer to eat only fresh vegetables. _____, when they are not available, I eat frozen or canned vegetables.

10. Have you read about the killing in the library last year? The police have been trying to solve that murder _____ for months, but so far they haven't been successful.

H. Topics FOR *Discussion* AND *Writing*

1. Work in small groups. The government has asked you to review the present procedure for arresting and booking a suspect. Review the steps involved in arresting and charging a person with a crime. Discuss what you would and would not change. Present your revised procedure to the class.

2. In the United States, trials are not held in secret. The public may sit in the courtroom and observe the proceedings. Visit a courtroom with two or three of your classmates. Observe what takes place. Report back to the class.

3. **Write in your journal.** Would you want to be part of a jury? Why or why not?

Follow-Up Activities

1. Refer to the chart in Exercise C, which lists the American procedure for arresting and trying a person for a crime. Compare this system with the system in your country. Using the following chart, compare the two systems, and write what you see as the advantages and disadvantages of each.

	In the United States	**In _____**
Procedure	Police arrest the suspect and read Miranda rights.	
Advantage		
Disadvantage		
Procedure		
Advantage		
Disadvantage		
Procedure		
Advantage		
Disadvantage		

2. Read about a criminal case in the news. Bring several newspaper and magazine articles on the case into class. In groups, form juries. Read through the evidence and decide whether the suspect is guilty or innocent. If your group decides the suspect is guilty, appoint a judge from your group to decide on a sentence.

CHAPTER 7: INNOCENT UNTIL PROVEN GUILTY: THE CRIMINAL COURT SYSTEM

Read the passage below. Fill in the blanks with one word from the list. Use each word only once.

appear	evidence	innocent	prove	time
consider	guilty	jury	punishment	whether
crime	hears	people	purpose	witnesses
defendant	however	protect	responsibility	words

The _____ of the American court system is to _____ the
         (1)   (2)

rights of the _____. According to American law, if someone is accused of a
          (3)

_____, he is considered _____ until the court proves that the per-
   (4)   (5)

son is guilty. In other _____, it is the responsibility of the court to
                     (6)

_____ that a person is _____. It is not the _____ of
   (7)   (8)   (9)

the person to prove that he is innocent.

At a trial, a jury of 12 men & women listens to the _____ from both attor-
                                                   (10)

neys and _____ the testimony of the _____. Then the
        (11)   (12)

_____ goes into a private room to _____ the evidence and decide
   (13)   (14)

_____ the defendant is guilty of the crime. If the jury decides that the
   (15)

_____ is innocent, he goes free. _____, if he is convicted, the
   (16)   (17)

judge sets a date for the defendant to _____ in court again for sentencing. At
                                   (18)

this _____, the judge tells the convicted person what his _____
     (19)   (20)

will be.

8

The Reliability of Eyewitnesses

Prereading Preparation

1. Look at the photograph. Where was this photograph taken? Who are the four women? Why are they there? Who are the two people sitting down? Who is the woman pointing to? Why?

2. What kinds of evidence are used to convict criminals? In small groups, use the chart below to make a list of the kinds of evidence used to convict criminals for the crimes listed.

Crime	Murder	Bank Robbery	Mugging
Types			
of			
Evidence			

3. In your country, what kinds of evidence are used to convict criminals for these crimes?

4. In your country, is an eyewitness's testimony important in convicting criminals?

5. In your opinion, what kinds of people make reliable eyewitnesses? Why?

The Reliability of Eyewitnesses

1   Bernard Jackson is a free man today, but he has many bitter memories.
2 Jackson spent five years in prison after a jury wrongly convicted him of raping
3 two women. At Jackson's trial, although two witnesses testified that Jackson
4 was with them in another location at the times of the crimes, he was convicted
5 anyway. Why? The jury believed the testimony of the two victims, who
6 positively identified Jackson as the man who had attacked them. The court
7 eventually freed Jackson after the police found the man who had really
8 committed the crimes. Jackson was similar in appearance to the guilty man. The
9 two women had made a mistake in identity. As a result, Jackson has lost five
10 years of his life.

11   The two women in this case were eyewitnesses. They clearly saw the man
12 who attacked them, yet they mistakenly identified an innocent person. Similar
13 incidents have occurred before. Eyewitnesses to other crimes have identified the
14 wrong person in a police lineup or in photographs.

15   Many factors influence the accuracy of eyewitness testimony. For instance,
16 witnesses sometimes see photographs of several suspects before they try to
17 identify the person they saw in a lineup of people. They can become confused by
18 seeing many photographs or similar faces. The number of people in the lineup,
19 and whether it is a live lineup or a photograph, may also affect a witness's
20 decision. People sometimes have difficulty identifying people of other races. The
21 questions the police ask witnesses also have an effect on them.

22   Are some witnesses more reliable than others? Many people believe that
23 police officers are more reliable than ordinary people. Psychologists decided to
24 test this idea, and they discovered that it is not true. Two psychologists showed
25 a film of crimes to both police officers and civilians. The psychologists found no
26 difference between the police and the civilians in correctly remembering the
27 details of the crimes.

28   Despite all the possibilities for inaccuracy, courts cannot exclude
29 eyewitness testimony from a trial. American courts depend almost completely
30 on eyewitness testimony to resolve court cases. Sometimes it is the only
31 evidence to a crime, such as rape. Furthermore, eyewitness testimony is often

32 correct. Although people do sometimes make mistakes, many times they really
33 do identify individuals correctly.
34   American courts depend on the ability of the 12 jurors, and not the judges,
35 to determine the accuracy of the witness's testimony. It is their responsibility to
36 decide if a certain witness could actually see, hear, and remember what occurred.
37   In a few cases, the testimony of eyewitnesses has convicted innocent people.
38 More importantly, it has rightly convicted a larger number of guilty people;
39 consequently, it continues to be of great value in the American judicial system.

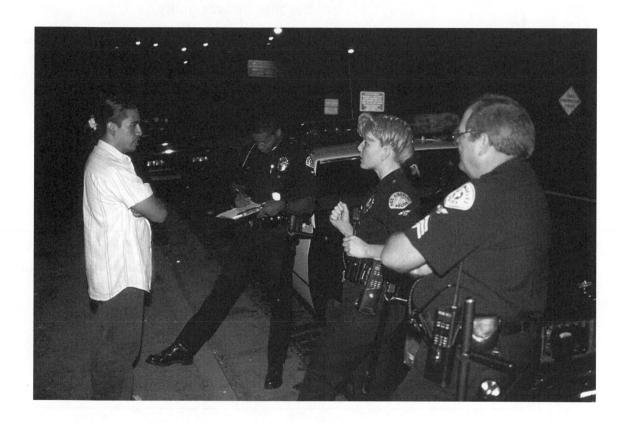

Read the passage again. Read the following statements. Check whether they are True or False. If a statement is false, rewrite the statement so that it is true. Then go back to the passage and find the line that supports your answer.

1. _____ True _____ False   Bernard Jackson went to jail for five years because he was guilty.

_____

2. _____ True _____ False   Bernard Jackson looked like the guilty man, but he was innocent.

_____

3. _____ True _____ False   The eyewitnesses in Jackson's trial were wrong.

_____

4. _____ True _____ False   Some witnesses become confused when they see too many photographs of similar people.

_____

5. _____ True _____ False   Police officers are better witnesses than ordinary people.

_____

6. _____ True _____ False   American courts depend a lot on eyewitness testimony.

_____

7. _____ True _____ False   The judge must decide if a witness's story is accurate.

_____

Reading Analysis

Read each question carefully. Either circle the letter of the correct answer, or write your answer in the space provided.

1. What is the main idea of the passage?
   a. Bernard Jackson spent five years in jail, but he was innocent.
   b. Eyewitness testimony, although sometimes incorrect, is valuable.
   c. Police officers are not better eyewitnesses than civilians.

2. According to the passage, which of the following factors influence eyewitnesses? Check the correct ones.
   _____ a. Seeing many similar photographs
   _____ b. The time of day the crime happened
   _____ c. The questions the police ask
   _____ d. The age and sex of the witness
   _____ e. A live lineup or a photograph of a group of people
   _____ f. The type of job the witness has
   _____ g. The education of the witness
   _____ h. The race of the suspect

3. Read lines 1–3. What are **bitter memories?**
   a. Angry memories
   b. Unhappy memories
   c. Prison memories

4. Read lines 5 and 6.
   a. What does **testimony** mean?
      1. A person's statement used for evidence
      2. A photograph used for evidence
      3. A clue used for evidence
   b. What does **victims** refer to?
      1. The people who commit a crime
      2. The people against whom a crime is committed

5. a. In line 12, what does **yet** mean?

    1. After

    2. So

    3. But

  b. How do you know?

    _____

6. In line 15, what does **for instance** mean?

  a. In addition

  b. For example

  c. However

7. Read lines 22–27: "…they discovered that it is not true."

  a. What is not true? It is not true that

    _____

  b. What are **civilians?**

    1. Police officers

    2. Ordinary people

    3. Psychologists

8. Read lines 28–33.

  a. What does **despite** mean?

    1. In addition to

    2. As a result

    3. In spite of

  b. What does **evidence** mean?

    1. Proof

    2. Result

    3. Story

9. Read lines 35 and 36: "It is their responsibility to decide if …." Who does **their** refer to?

  a. The judges

  b. The courts

  c. The jurors

10. Read lines 38 and 39. What does **consequently** mean?
    a. As a result
    b. However
    c. In addition

Refer to the wanted poster above. In small groups, answer the following questions.

1. Who is this man?

2. Who drew this picture?

3. What do the police think this man did?

4. Where can you see wanted posters?

Information Organization

Read the passage again. Underline what you think are the main ideas. Then scan the reading and complete the following outline, using the sentences that you have underlined to help you. You will use this outline later to answer questions about the reading.

I.   Bernard Jackson's Case

    A.   His Crime:

    B.   The Evidence:

    C.   Reason for His Conviction:

    D.   The Problem:

II. Factors Influencing the Accuracy of Eyewitness Testimony

    A.

    B.

    C.

    D.

    E.   The questions the police ask witnesses have an effect on them.

III. Experiment to Test the Reliability of Police Officers and Ordinary People as Witnesses

    A.   Experiment:

    B.   Results:

IV. Why Courts Cannot Exclude Eyewitness Testimony from a Trial

    A.

    B.

Information Recall and Summary

Read each question carefully. Use your outline to answer the questions. Do not refer back to the passage. When you are finished, write a brief summary of the reading.

1. Why did Bernard Jackson go to prison? Was he guilty?

   _____

2. At Jackson's trial, what did the two witnesses testify? Did the jury believe the two witnesses?

   _____

   _____

3. Why did the victims identify Jackson as the man who had attacked them?

   _____

4. What are some factors that affect eyewitness testimony?

   _____

   _____

5. a. Are police officers better witnesses than ordinary people?

      _____

   b. How did psychologists test this idea?

      _____

6. Why is eyewitness testimony important in an American court?

   _____

7. In an American court, who decides if the eyewitness testimony is correct or not? Why is eyewitness testimony a valuable part of the American judicial system?

_____

_____

Summary

Work in pairs or alone. Write a brief summary of the reading, and put it on the blackboard. Compare your summary with your classmates'. Which one best describes the main idea of the reading?

_____

_____

_____

_____

Word Forms

PART 1

In English, there are several ways verbs change to nouns. Some verbs become nouns by adding the suffix *-ence* or *-ance*—for example, *insist (v.)* becomes *insistence (n.)*.

Complete each sentence with the correct form of the words on the left. **Use the correct tense of the verb in either the affirmative or the negative form. Use the singular or plural form of the noun.**

depend *(v.)*
dependence *(n.)*

1. a. When a baby is born, it _____ on its parents completely.
    b. As it grows up, the child's _____ on its parents decreases.

differ *(v.)*
difference *(n.)*

2. a. Angela's coat and Debbie's coat _____ in color. They are both blue.
    b. The only _____ between the two coats are their size and material.

occur *(v.)*
occurrence *(n.)*

3. a. Snow in April is an unusual _____ in this area.
    b. In fact, snow _____ very often, even in the winter. Only two or three inches fall during the entire season.

appear *(v.)*
appearance *(n.)*

4. a. The President made a special _____ on television last night.
    b. He _____ very calm, but his news was serious.

assist *(v.)*
assistance *(n.)*

5. a. The nurses _____ the doctor today, but they will help her during the operation tomorrow.
    b. The doctor will need their _____ to give her surgical instruments.

In English, the verb and noun forms of some words are the same—for example, *change (n.)* and *change (v.)*.

Complete each sentence with the correct form of the word on the left. **Use the correct tense of the verb in either the affirmative or the negative form. Use the singular or plural form of the noun. In addition, indicate whether you are using the noun (n.) or verb (v.) form.**

influence

1. a. Many people believe that the weather _____ our feelings. *(n., v.)*

   b. However the strength of this _____ has not been proven. *(n., v.)*

film

2. a. Unfortunately, John _____ our high school reunion next month. *(n., v.)*

   b. His _____ of social gatherings are always *(n., v.)*

      interesting, so we are very disappointed.

attack

3. a. People frequently write _____ on politicians in *(n., v.)*

      the newspapers, but the politicians do not always pay attention to them.

   b. People usually _____ the politicians' dishonesty. *(n., v.)*

witness

4. a. Margaret was the only _____ to a serious car accident. *(n., v.)*

   b. As soon as she _____ the accident, she called an *(n., v.)*

      ambulance and the police.

mistake   5.   a.   Susan and Emily are twin sisters. People frequently

_____ Emily for Susan and Susan for Emily
(n., v.)
because they look alike.

b.   Sometimes such _____ in identity are funny.
(n., v.)

question   6.   a.   The police _____ the suspect until his lawyer
(n., v.)

arrived. The suspect wanted his lawyer to be present.

b.   They asked him very specific _____, but his
(n., v.)
answers were unclear.

F. DICTIONARY SKILLS

Read the following sentences. Use the context to help you understand the boldface words. Read the dictionary entry for that word and circle the appropriate definition. Then rewrite the sentence, using the definition you have chosen. Be sure to make your sentence grammatically correct.

1. The number of people in the **lineup,** and whether it is a live lineup or a photograph, may affect a witness's decision.

> **lineup** /ˈlaɪnˌʌp/ *n.* **1** (in baseball) a list of players in the order in which they will come to bat. **2** *fig.* any listing of people, events, products, etc. **3** a group of people, including criminal suspects, presented by police to witnesses who try to identify the criminal(s) in the group.

_____

_____

2. Courts cannot **exclude** eyewitness testimony from a trial. Sometimes it is the only evidence to a crime.

> **exclude** /ɛkˈsklud/ *v.* [T] **-cluded, -cluding, -cludes 1** not to include, leave out, *(syn.)* to omit. **2** to keep out, *(syns.)* to prohibit, ban.

_____

_____

3. Eyewitness testimony continues to be of **value** in the American judicial system.

> **value** /ˈvælyu/ *n.* **1** [U] worth. **2** [U] liking, importance. **3** *pl.* ideal, standards of a society.

_____

_____

4. The two women were **positive** that Bernard Jackson had committed the crimes against them.

> **positive** /pazətɪv/ *adj.* **1** optimistic, hopeful. **2** certain, definite, without doubt. **3** indicating yes. **4** helpful, beneficial.

_____

_____

Vocabulary in Context

bitter *(adj.)*	guilty *(adj.)*	similar *(adj.)*
civilian *(n.)*	innocent *(adj.)*	testimony *(n.)*
despite *(prep.)*	mistake *(n.)*	victims *(n.)*
evidence *(n.)*		

Read the following sentences. Complete each blank space with the correct word from the list above. Use each word only once.

1. John was in the army for two years. At the end of his military service, he was happy to become a _____ again.

2. Last week, an armed robber shot two men when he robbed the City Bank. Afterwards, an ambulance took the two _____ to the hospital.

3. Tommy stole a car, but the police caught and arrested him. Because Tommy was _____, he went to prison for six months.

4. Kathy saw the two men who robbed City Bank. As a result of her _____ in court, the two men were convicted and put into prison.

5. When the police investigate a crime, they look for _____, such as fingerprints, footprints, hair, and clothing.

6. Mr. Michaels worked for the same company for 25 years. Six months before retiring, he lost his job, and he couldn't find another one. He has become very _____ towards his old company.

7. Many people believed that Ronald had murdered his wife, but he was _____.

8. _____ the cold weather, Kay went to work without her coat.

9. Chris and his brother look very _____. They are both tall and thin, and both have light hair and blue eyes.

10. The waitress made a _____. She gave me coffee, but I had ordered tea.

H. Topics FOR *Discussion* AND *Writing*

1. In this article, the two women made a mistake in identity. Think about a case you know of in which an innocent person was convicted of a crime because eyewitnesses made a mistake. Describe the case.

2. Is it possible to be sure of an eyewitness's testimony? Please explain.

3. **Write in your journal.** Have you ever witnessed a crime or an accident? Were you able to remember the exact details? Why or why not? Describe what happened.

Follow-Up Activities

1. Reread lines 15–21 of the article. What can the police do differently to help avoid cases of mistaken identity? With a partner, read the following sets of questions. Decide which one in each pair is the better question for the police to ask. Compare your choices with your classmates' choices. Be prepared to explain your decisions.

   a. _____ 1. What was the suspect wearing?

   _____ 2. Was the suspect wearing a shirt and pants, or a suit?

   b. _____ 1. Did the suspect have a gun or a knife?

   _____ 2. Did the suspect have a weapon? If so, what did you see?

   c. _____ 1. Exactly what did the suspect look like? Describe the suspect's face in detail.

   _____ 2. Will you look at these photographs and tell us which one is a photo of the suspect?

   d. _____ 1. What do you estimate was the suspect's height and weight?

   _____ 2. How tall and heavy was the suspect?

2. In this article, the two women made a mistake in identity. There are many factors that can cause people to make an error. Refer to the chart below. Work in small groups with your classmates. Which factors might confuse people and cause them to make mistakes in identity? Why? Write your reasons and rank the factors in the table below. For example, if you think that **weather** is the factor that would confuse people the most, write **1** next to **weather** under **RANK.**

FACTOR	REASON	RANK
sex (of witness/ of suspect)		
race (of witness/ of suspect)		
age (of witness/ of suspect)		
time of day		
weather		
distance of witness from the crime		
level of education of the witness		

CHAPTER 8: THE RELIABILITY OF EYEWITNESSES

Read the passage below. Fill in the blanks with one word from the list. Use each word only once.

appearance	despite	influence	mistake	similar
bitter	evidence	innocent	occurred	testimony
civilians	eyewitness	instance	questions	victims
crimes	guilty	judges	reliable	yet

Bernard Jackson is a free man today, but he has many _____ memories.
(1)
Jackson spent five years in prison after a jury convicted him of raping two women.
Jackson's lawyer introduced witnesses who testified that Jackson was with them in another
location at the times of the crimes. Why, then, was he convicted? The jury believed the

_____ of the two _____. They positively identified Jackson as the
(2)   (3)
man who had attacked them. The court eventually freed Jackson after the police found the

man who had really committed the crimes. Jackson was similar in _____ to
(4)
the guilty man. The two women had made a _____ in identity. As a result,
(5)
Jackson has lost five years of his life.

The two women in this case were eyewitnesses. They clearly saw the man who

attacked them, _____ they mistakenly identified an innocent person. Similar
(6)
incidents have _____ before. Eyewitnesses to other crimes have identified the
(7)
wrong person in a police lineup or in photographs.

Many factors _____the accuracy of eyewitness testimony. For
(8)
_____, witnesses sometimes see photographs of several suspects before they
(9)
try to identify the person they saw in a lineup of people. They can become confused by

seeing many photographs of _____ faces. The number of people in the lineup,
                                        (10)
and whether it is a live lineup or a photograph, may also affect a witness's decision. People
sometimes have difficulty identifying people of other races. The _____ the
                                                                            (11)
police ask witnesses also have an effect on them.

Are some witnesses more _____ than others? Many people believe that
                                    (12)
police officers are more accurate than ordinary people. Psychologists decided to test this
idea, and they discovered that it is not true. Two psychologists showed a film of
_____ to both police officers and _____. The psychologists found
        (13)   (14)
no difference between the two groups in correctly remembering the details of the crimes.

_____ all the possibilities for inaccuracy, courts cannot exclude eyewit-
        (15)
ness testimony from a trial. American courts almost completely depend on eyewitness testimony to resolve court cases. Sometimes it is the only _____ to a crime, such
                                                                    (16)
as rape. Furthermore, _____ testimony is often correct. Although people do
                                (17)
sometimes make mistakes, many times they really do identify individuals correctly.

American courts depend on the ability of the twelve jurors, and not the
_____, to determine the accuracy of the witness's testimony. It is their respon-
        (18)
sibility to decide if a certain witness could actually see, hear, and remember what occurred.

In a few cases, the testimony of eyewitnesses has convicted _____ people.
                                                                            (19)
More importantly, it has rightly convicted a larger number of _____ people;
                                                                        (20)
consequently, it continues to be a valuable part of the American judicial system.

9

Solving Crime with Modern Technology

Prereading Preparation

1. Work in a small group. What types of technology can help solve crimes? Make a list. When you are finished, share your list with the class.

Type of Technology	How can this help solve a crime?

2. Who are the different people that solve crimes? How are their jobs different from each other's jobs? How do they try to solve crimes?

Solving Crimes with Modern Technology

1   Solving crimes is one of the most important jobs of law enforcement.

2 Improvements in crime technology help detectives solve crimes faster, and more

3 efficiently, today. For example, crime labs have new kinds of DNA testing,

4 which can identify body fluids such as blood, sweat, and saliva. There are also

5 new kinds of fingerprint testing. In the past, fingerprint testing was only

6 helpful if the fingerprints from the crime scene could be matched with "prints"

7 that were already on file. The fingerprints of convicted criminals are kept on file

8 in police records permanently. People whose fingerprints are not on file cannot

9 be identified in this way, and as a result, many crimes have not been solved.

10   However, the newest kind of fingerprint testing can do much more than

11 simply record a fingerprint pattern. It can provide additional information about

12 a fingerprint, such as the age and sex of its owner. The fingerprints can reveal if

13 the person takes medication, too. But the latest technology does even more. It

14 can even get fingerprints from fabric, for example, from blankets or curtains.

15   In a recent case, the police in Tacoma, Washington, found the body of a 27-

16 year-old woman who had been murdered in her bedroom. There were no

17 witnesses, and her apartment had few clues. The only real evidence did not

18 seem very helpful. The victim's bed sheet had some of her blood on it and

19 looked as if someone had wiped his or her hands. At the time of the murder, it

20 was impossible to identify a fingerprint, or even a palm print, from fabric. This

21 is because all the unique characteristics of fingerprints and palm prints can get

22 lost in a fabric. The detectives were unable to use the evidence, but they saved it

23 anyway. Then they called Eric Berg, a forensic expert with the Tacoma police, for

24 help. A forensic expert is a person who helps solve crimes.

25   Eric Berg was not only a forensic expert, but a computer expert, too. Using

26 his own time and money, he had already spent years developing computer

27 software in his own home to enhance, or improve, crime scene photos. He

28 decided to use that software to examine the fabric from the murder case. It

29 worked! Eric Berg had used his computer to make the palm print more

30 apparent, or clear. When he was done, he gave the evidence to the detectives.

31 The detectives found a man whose palm print matched a print on file. Only two

32 hours later, the suspect was arrested. He was eventually convicted of the crime

33 and is now in jail. Today, many other police departments use Eric Berg's new

34 software. Because of it, crimes that seemed to be unsolvable were suddenly

35 solvable again.

36   While all of this technology may help solve future crimes, they may also

37 help solve crimes from the past. In all crimes, detectives carefully take samples

38 of evidence from the scene. In many cases 15 or 20 years ago, the police could

39 not always identify important evidence such as body fluids. In these cases, they

40 stored the evidence in a freezer. Now, criminologists have the modern

technology they require to examine the frozen evidence, and, in many cases, identify it as well. In Newport News, Virginia, detectives today are reinvestigating a 15-year-old murder case. A 34-year-old woman was murdered, and a pair of scissors was found at the crime scene. The police had only one clue: the scissors. The police found a drop of sweat on the scissors, but they had no way of studying it because, at the time, the DNA technology was not very advanced. Today, however, they are using the new DNA technology and believe it may lead them to the murderer.

Today, police have other kinds of new crime-solving technology, as well. A laser system of lights helps detectives find evidence of body fluids at a crime scene in daylight. Previously, it was only possible to see this kind of evidence at night or in the dark. By helping the police identify criminals, this new technology can help put more criminals in prison.

Fact-Finding Exercise

Read the passage again. Read the following statements. Check whether they are True or False. If a statement is false, rewrite the statement so that it is true. Then go back to the passage and find the line that supports your answer.

1. _____ True _____ False   Fingerprint testing always helps to solve crimes.

_____

2. _____ True _____ False   New fingerprint technology can identify body fluids.

_____

3. _____ True _____ False   When the woman was murdered in Tacoma, Washington, it was impossible to identify a fingerprint from fabric.

_____

4. _____ True _____ False   Eric Berg quickly developed new software to improve photos.

_____

5. _____ True _____ False   Eric Berg's technology may help solve older crimes, too.

_____

6. _____ True _____ False   The drop of sweat on the scissors was the only clue in the Virginia murder.

_____

7. _____ True _____ False   The laser system of lights can only find evidence in the dark.

_____

Reading Analysis

Read each question carefully. Either circle the letter of the correct answer, or write your answer in the space provided.

1. What is the main idea of the passage?
   a. New technology always solves every crime, even old ones.
   b. New technology helps solve many crimes, even old ones.
   c. New technology is only useful in solving murders.

2. Read lines 3–8.
   a. What are **blood, sweat,** and **saliva?**

   _____

   b. How do you know?

   _____

   c. Why is the word **prints** in quotation marks (" ")?
      1. Because it is an abbreviated form of the word *fingerprints*
      2. Because it is an unusual word in criminal investigation
      3. Because it may be confused with prints of photographs
   d. Whose prints are **"already on file"?**
      1. People who have never committed a crime in the past
      2. People who have been convicted of a crime in the past
      3. All the people who live in a city, state, or country

3. Read lines 13 and 14.
   a. What are **blankets** and **curtains?**

   _____

   b. How do you know?

   _____

4. Read lines 16–18. Which word is a synonym for **clues?**

   _____

5. Read lines 22–27.

    a. What is a **forensic expert?**

    _____

    b. An **expert** is a person who
       1. is very skilled at working with evidence
       2. is very skilled at working with computers
       3. is very skilled at working in a special field

    c. What does **enhance** mean?

    _____

    d. How do you know?

    _____

6. Read lines 35–39.

    a. In the past, what did the police sometimes do with evidence they could not identify?
       1. They threw it away.
       2. They didn't collect it.
       3. They saved it.

    b. Why did they do this?

    _____

7. Read lines 41–43.

    a. What was the only clue the police had in the 15-year-old murder case?

    _____

    b. What is the purpose of the colon (:) in line 44?
       a. It introduces the clue.
       b. It connects two sentences.
       c. It separates two ideas.

8. Read lines 48–51. What does **previously** mean?
    a. Unfortunately
    b. In the past
    c. Surprisingly

Information Organization

Read the passage a second time. Underline what you think are the main ideas. Then scan the reading and complete the following chart, using the sentences that you have underlined to help you. You will use this chart later to answer questions about the reading.

Type of Technology	1. Fingerprint Testing	2. DNA Testing	3. Laser Lights
How can it help solve crimes?			
Which crime was it useful for?			
Why was it useful?			

Read each question carefully. Use your outline to answer the questions. Do not refer back to the passage. When you are finished, write a brief summary of the reading.

1. a. What can new fingerprint testing identify about a criminal?

    _____

    _____

    b. How is this different from fingerprint testing in the past?

    _____

    _____

2. Why is it difficult to identify a fingerprint or palm print on fabric?

    _____

    _____

3. How can new DNA testing help solve the crime in Newport News, Virginia?

    _____

    _____

4. Why is laser light technology important?

    _____

    _____

Summary

Work in pairs or alone. Write a brief summary of the reading, and put it on the blackboard. Compare your summary with your classmates'. Which one best describes the main idea of the reading?

_____

_____

_____

_____

_____

PART 1

In English, some verbs change to nouns by adding *-ment,* for example, *arrange (v.),* *arrangement (n.).*

Complete each sentence with a correct form of the words on the left. **Use the correct tense of the verb in either the affirmative or the negative. Use the singular or plural form of the noun.**

improve *(v.)*
improvement *(n.)*

1. a. Criminologists have made many _____ in the ways they now solve crimes.
    b. Criminologists _____ the accuracy of their work only to catch criminals. They also try to help prove that some suspects are innocent, too.

enhance *(v.)*
enhancement *(n.)*

2. a. Jane put on her makeup very carefully. She believes that makeup _____ her appearance.
    b. Sam doesn't think that Jane's appearance needs _____. He thinks she's very pretty without makeup.

enforce *(v.)*
enforcement *(n.)*

3. a. One of a police officer's jobs is law _____.
    b. A police officer not only _____ the law, but also tries to help prevent crimes from happening.

develop *(v.)*
development *(n.)*

4. a. Many people work for years on the effective _____ of new computer software.
    b. People usually _____ simple software programs. They prefer to work on complex and powerful software programs.

require *(v.)*
requirement *(n.)*

5. a. Michelle wanted to work for a new company, but the company _____ a Master's degree in business, and she didn't have one.
    b. Michelle returned to school and studied for her Master's degree in order to meet the company's education _____.

PART 2

In English, the verb and noun forms of some words are the same—for example, *help (n.)* and *help (v.)*.

Complete each sentence with the correct form of the word on the left. **Use the correct tense of the verb in either the affirmative or the negative form. Use the singular or plural form of the noun. In addition, indicate whether you are using the noun *(n.)* or verb *(v.)* form.**

witness   1.   a.   When a couple gets married, they need to have _____
                        who attend the marriage ceremony.   *(n., v.)*

             b.   The people who _____ the marriage ceremony sign
                                         (n., v.)
                   their names on a legal document.

file   2.   a.   The police keep_____ on all convicted criminals.
                                      (n., v.)

                   They have fingerprints, photographs, and other information
                   about each person.

             b.   They _____ the information in unlocked cabinets.
                        (n., v.)
                   They keep the information carefully locked away.

murder   3.   a.   The law classifies _____ into several categories,
                                        (n., v.)
                   depending on whether the killing was planned, unplanned, or
                   accidental, for example.

             b.   Every _____ is carefully investigated.
                        (n., v.)

arrest   4.   a.   Tomorrow the police _____ a suspect in a "white
                                           (n., v.)
                   collar" crime. The person is suspected of stealing company
                   secrets and selling them to another company.

             b.   The number of _____ involving white
                                  (n., v.)
                   collar crime has increased dramatically in recent years.

record   5.   a.   Doctors and dentists _____ their patients' health

(n., v.)

history for permanent reference.

     b.   Such health _____ can be very helpful.

(n., v.)

F. DICTIONARY SKILLS

Read the following sentences. Use the context to help you understand the boldface words. Read the dictionary entry for that word and circle the appropriate definition. Then rewrite the sentence, using the definition you have chosen. Be sure to make your sentence grammatically correct.

1. The latest technology can even get fingerprints from **fabric**, for example, blankets or curtains.

> **fabric** *n* **1** cloth material: *The sofa is covered with a soft cotton ~.* **2** the composition, substance of something: *The ~ of our society has been torn by crime and a bad economy.*

_____

_____

2. The newest kind of fingerprint testing can do much more than simply record a fingerprint **pattern.**

> **pattern** *n* **1** an example or model to be followed: *Her writing shows a ~ of excellence.* **2** a form or guide to follow when making something: *She made the dress herself from a ~.* **3** a design of regular shapes and lines: *The flower ~ in that dress is very pretty.* **4** a repeated set of events, characteristics, or features: *There is a ~ to his behavior.*

_____

_____

3. In all crimes, detectives carefully take samples of evidence from the **scene.**

> **scene** *n* **1 a** a piece of film or play, usually showing one situation: *There is a very exciting chase ~ in that movie.* **b** part of an act: *Let's rehearse Act II, ~ 2.* **2** anger or embarrassing behavior, often in public: *She made a ~ at the party by drinking too much and falling into the swimming pool.* **3** a place where something happens: *the crime scene.* **4** a view of something, especially from a specific place: *She won a prize for her photo of a country ~.*

_____

_____

arrests (n.)	evidence (v.)	file (n.)
clues (n.)	experts (n.)	pattern (n.)
criminologists (n.)	fabric (n.)	scene (n.)
enforce (v.)		

Read the sentences below. Complete each blank space with the correct word from the list above. Use each word only once.

1. Police officers, detectives, and many other people _____ the law in a variety of ways.

2. Much _____ is required in order to identify a suspect and solve a crime.

3. We always _____ our important documents in a safe place.

4. Michael wanted to ask Jane to marry him. The _____ he chose for his proposal was the restaurant where they had dinner together for the first time.

5. _____ such as hair and skin provide very good evidence for identifying crime suspects.

6. The complex _____ on that carpet is very attractive.

7. Some mechanics are _____ at finding out what is wrong with a car.

8. Cotton is a very cool _____ to wear in the heat of the summer.

9. _____ are very skilled at solving crimes.

10. The police can only make _____ when they have enough evidence to suspect someone of having committed a crime.

H. Topics FOR Discussion AND Writing

1. In the United States, the fingerprints of convicted criminals are kept on file permanently. Do you agree with this? Or do you think the fingerprints should not be on file after the criminal comes out of jail? Why? Explain your opinion.

2. Criminal investigators try to collect as much evidence as they can in order to identify the person who committed a crime. How much evidence does a jury need in order to convict a person of a crime?

3. Many people's fingerprints are not on file. As a result, criminal investigators cannot always use fingerprints they find at the scene of a crime. These fingerprints may not be on file. Should the law require all people to put their fingerprints on file, even if they have never committed a crime? Explain your reasons for your answer.

4. **Write in your journal.** Chapter 9 discusses some new kinds of technology to help solve crimes. Which new technology do you think is the most important one? Why? What types of crimes do you think it can help solve?

Follow-Up Activities

1. Each person's fingerprints are unique and do not change over the person's lifetime. Scientists studied fingerprint patterns and developed a system for classifying them by type in order to make identification more accurate. Examine the sample fingerprints below.

Figure 1: Arch

Figure 2: Left Loop

Figure 3: Right Loop

Figure 4: Tent

Figure 5: Whorl

On a separate sheet of paper, make your own fingerprint and compare it to the samples. Which pattern does your fingerprint have? How is it similar to that pattern? What are the differences that make it clear they are not the same fingerprint?

When you have finished, be sure to destroy the paper with your fingerprint on it.

2. Go to www.nist.gov/public_affairs/licweb/fingerprints.htm and examine the sample prints. Then do the fingerprint matching game. See if you can identify the print taken from a crime scene.

3. Read the line graph below. Answer the questions that follow.

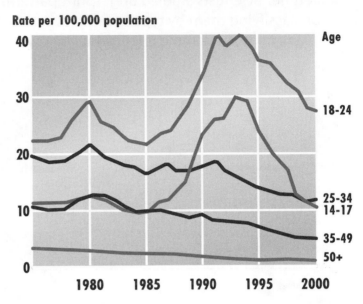

Homicide Offending by Age, 1976-2000

Rate per 100,000 population

a. In which five-year period were the most homicides committed?
   1. 1980–1985   3. 1990–1995
   2. 1985–1990   4. 1995–2000

b. For all five-year time periods, how old is the person most likely to have committed a homicide?

   _____

c. For all five-year time periods, how old is the person least likely to have committed a homicide?

   _____

d. What can we conclude from this graph?
   1. As people get older, they are more likely to commit a homicide.
   2. As people get older, they are less likely to commit a homicide.
   3. As people get older, they are still equally likely to commit a homicide.

4. Read the following line graph. Answer the questions that follow.

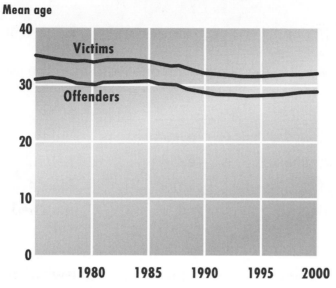

Average Age of Homicide Victims and Offenders, 1976-2000

a. Who is a **victim?**

    1. The person who is killed
    2. The killer

b. Who is an **offender?**

    1. The person who is killed
    2. The killer

c. From 1980 to 2000, what can you understand about the age of a homicide victim and the age of the victim's killer?

    1. The difference between their ages increased.
    2. The difference between their ages decreased.
    3. The difference between their ages remained about the same.

d. For the 20-year time period indicated on the chart, what can you understand about the age of homicide victims and the age of their killer?

    1. The homicide victims and their killers are about the same age.
    2. The homicide victims are usually older than their killers.
    3. The homicide victims are usually younger than their killers.

CHAPTER 9: SOLVING CRIME WITH MODERN TECHNOLOGY

Read the passage below. Fill in the blanks with one word from the list. Use each word only once.

additional	crime	evidence	fluids	reveal
apparent	criminals	expert	helpful	solved
arrested	efficiently	fabric	identify	technology
clues	enhance	file	matched	witnesses

Solving crimes is one of the most important jobs of law enforcement.

Improvements in _____ technology help detectives solve crimes faster, and
(1)

more _____, today. For example, crime labs have new kinds of DNA testing,
(2)

which can identify body _____ such as blood, sweat, and saliva. There are also
(3)

new kinds of fingerprint testing. In the past, fingerprint testing was only

_____ if the fingerprints from the crime scene could be _____
(4)   (5)

with "prints" that were already on file. The fingerprints of convicted _____ are
(6)

kept on file in police records permanently. People whose fingerprints are not on

_____ cannot be identified in this way, and as a result, many crimes have not
(7)

been _____.
(8)

However, the newest kind of fingerprint testing can do much more than simply

record a fingerprint pattern. It can provide _____ information about a finger-
(9)

print, such as the age and sex of its owner. The fingerprints can _____ if the
(10)

person takes medication, too. But the latest _____ does even more. It can
(11)

even get fingerprints from _____, for example, blankets or curtains.
(12)

In a recent case, the police in Tacoma, Washington, found the body of a 27-year-old
woman who had been murdered in her bedroom. There were no _____, and
(13)

her apartment had few _____. The only real evidence did not seem very
(14)

helpful. The victim's bed sheet had some of her blood on it and looked as if someone had
wiped his hands. At the time of the murder, it was impossible to _____ a
(15)

fingerprint from fabric. The detectives were unable to use the _____, but they
(16)

saved it anyway. Then they called Eric Berg. He was not only a forensic expert, but a
computer _____, too. He had spent years developing computer software in
(17)

his own home to _____, or improve, crime scene photos. Eric Berg had used his
(18)

computer to make the palm print more _____, or clear. When he was done, he
(19)

gave the evidence to the detectives. The detectives found a man whose palm print
matched a print on file. Only two hours later the suspect was _____. He was
(20)

eventually convicted of the crime and is now in jail.

K.   Crossword Puzzle

Read the clues on the next page. Write the answers in the correct spaces in the puzzle.

Crossword Puzzle Clues

Across

3. During a trial, people give _____. They say what they saw or know about the case.

5. If a person is _____ of a crime, the jury acquits him.

8. _____ is money that the suspect gives the court to ensure that he or she will appear in court again.

10. If a person is proven _____, then she is convicted.

12. However; nevertheless

14. An error

19. Improve; make better

20. There are different types of _____ for a crime; for example, fines, probation, and time in prison.

21. Need

23. In the past; before

25. A _____ is a person who saw a crime take place.

Down

1. The word _____ is an abbreviated form of the word fingerprints.

2. I like to write with a _____. I don't like pencils.

4. An _____ is a person who is skilled in a particular area.

6. The jury needs strong _____ to prove that a suspect really committed a crime.

7. Blood, saliva, and sweat are all body _____.

8. The police record the charges against a suspect at the police station. They _____ the suspect.

9. A _____ is the person a crime is committed against.

11. Dependability

13. Cloth such as a blanket, curtains, or clothing

15. A _____ is the punishment that the judge gives a convicted person.

Down (continued)

16. **I, _____ ; he, him**

17. Part of a police officer's job is to _____ the law.

18. If a suspect cannot afford a lawyer, the judge may _____ one.

22. The opposite of **"yes"**

24. The opposite of **"down"**

The three chapters in this unit all discuss an aspect of crime. Chapter 7 outlines how a suspect is arrested and charged with a crime. Chapter 8 describes how an innocent man was convicted as a result of eyewitnesses' mistakes. Chapter 9 discusses how modern technology can help solve crimes.

1. Should lawmakers and the courts consider such factors as a criminal's home life, age, and physical condition when making laws and punishing convicted criminals?

2. Can courts ensure that eyewitnesses have not made mistakes? If so, how?

3. How much evidence is needed in order to convict a suspect of a crime and be sure the guilty person is truly guilty?

1. Have you ever witnessed or been in a car or bus accident ? Did the police investigate using forensic evidence? Describe how they gathered information about the accident. Was it clear who was guilty and who was innocent in the accident?

2. Read the questions and then watch the video once or twice. Circle the correct answer.

   1. The first accident on the video involved _____.

      a. an airplane   b. a train   c. a helicopter   d. a car

   2. Judges and juries feel _____ with video evidence.

      a. nervous   b. comfortable   c. discouraged   d. significant

   3. Arthur Ginsburg's company has been making computer animations for _____ years.

      a. five   b. ten   c fifteen   d. twenty

   4. Which vehicle is not involved in an accident in the video?

      a. utility cart   b. bicycle   c car   d. bus

   5. A forensic video usually costs between _____ thousand dollars to create.

      a. 5 and 10   b. 10 and 20   c. 20 and 30   d. 30 and 40

3. Why don't computer animations of accidents show faces or graphic details of the crash scenes? Do you think this is a fair way for juries to judge guilt or innocence?

 Surfing THE **INTERNET**

Search the Internet for "Forensic Animation". When you find a good web site, search again for information about the process of creating forensic animation for "car accidents." Print out or save any interesting information to share with your class.

Optional Activity: Search the Internet for the name of your city or town and the word "police" or "crime". Share any interesting statistics or information you might find. Look for information about community anti-crime programs or, if it interests you, employment opportunities in law enforcement.

*Forensic = related to the use of science to investigate a legal problem.

UNIT 4

SCIENCE AND HISTORY

10

Ancient Artifacts and Ancient Air

Prereading Preparation

1. What kind of work do archeologists perform?

2. What do archeologists study in order to learn about the past?

3. What can archeological discoveries tell us about the past?

4. Where would you find ancient air?

5. How can ancient air help us learn about the past? About the future?

Ancient Artifacts and Ancient Air

Archeologists made an exciting discovery in Egypt in 1954. During an excavation near the base of the Great Pyramid, they uncovered an ancient crypt. Although they believed that this discovery would help us understand Egypt's past, they also hoped that it would give us important information about the future.

This crypt was a tomb, or burial place, for a dead Egyptian pharaoh, or king. Historians believed that the Egyptians buried their pharaohs with two boats: one to carry the body and the other to carry the soul. This was one of their religious customs about death. The archeologists expected to find two boats inside the crypt. As they broke the crypt open, they smelled the scent of wood. The ancient Egyptians had sealed the room so effectively that the aroma of the cedar wood was still preserved. Inside the crypt, archeologists found a 4,600-year-old boat that was in almost perfect condition. In addition, they found another closed room next to the crypt. Archeologists and historians believed that this chamber contained the second boat. If so, archeologists would have better information about the past. They would be sure about the religious custom of burying pharaohs with two boats.

However, this was not the only information they hoped to find. They wondered if the air in the two rooms contained something special that helped to preserve the wood. This information could help in the preservation of ancient artifacts in museums throughout the world. Researchers also hoped to find some answers about the future by carefully examining the air in the second chamber. When the archeologists opened the first chamber, all the old air escaped. Scientists wanted to recover the air in the second chamber, compare it with the air of the present, and then examine the differences, especially differences in the level of carbon dioxide (CO_2). This information might help them predict changes in the air in the future. They also did not want outside air to get inside the chamber. Careful planning would be necessary in order to open the second room and save the air. In fact, it took years to plan the excavation and to design and make the equipment necessary to open the chamber and collect the air inside.

Finally, in October 1986 an international team of scientists, using special equipment, drilled through the roof of the chamber. The hole they made was kept carefully sealed. As they broke into the ancient room, they realized that the chamber was not sealed. They took an air sample. The air inside was the same as the air outside. The scientists were very disappointed. However, they continued working to see what was inside the chamber. The team lowered a light and a camera into the small hole, and looked at the interior of the room on a television monitor. The second boat was really there!

40   After the scientists took samples of the air inside the chamber and
41 photographed it completely, they sealed up the hole in the roof and left the
42 room as they had found it. Although they did not get samples of 4,600-year-
43 old air, they did confirm the Egyptian custom of burying pharaohs with two
44 boats. More importantly, they practiced a new, nondestructive approach to
45 archeology: investigate an ancient location, photograph it, and leave it
46 untouched. When archeologists opened the first chamber, they removed the
47 boat. The Egyptian government built a museum on the site for the first boat.
48 During the construction of the museum, the vibrations from the heavy
49 machinery disturbed the second room and probably destroyed the seal. Water
50 leaked in, too, so the second boat was not as well preserved as the first boat.

51   The investigation of the second chamber taught archeologists a valuable
52 lesson. New excavations will not only use modern technology, but they will also
53 follow the idea of preserving the entire location for future studies.

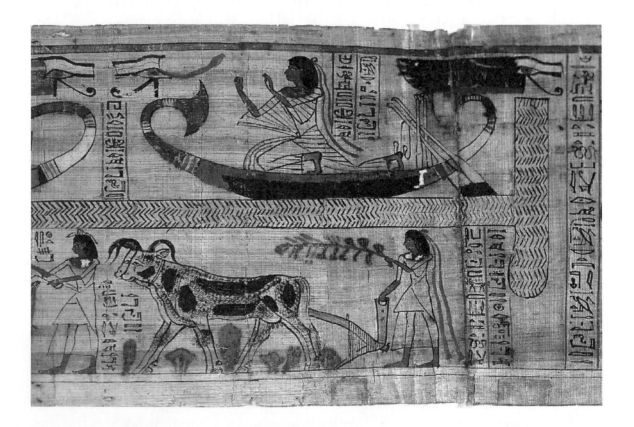

Fact-Finding Exercise

Read the passage again. Read the following statements. Check whether they are True or False. If a statement is false, rewrite the statement so that it is true. Then go back to the passage and find the line that supports your answer.

1. ____ True ____ False   Archeological discoveries give us information about the past.

_____

2. ____ True ____ False   Archeologists recently discovered a body in a crypt in Egypt.

_____

3. ____ True ____ False   Archeologists found a boat in the second crypt near the Great Pyramids.

_____

4. ____ True ____ False   Archeologists have not opened the second room yet.

_____

5. ____ True ____ False   There is no old air left in the second chamber.

_____

6. ____ True ____ False   The investigation team went inside the second chamber.

_____

7. ____ True ____ False   The Egyptian government is going to put the second boat in a museum.

_____

Read each question carefully. Either circle the letter of the correct answer, or write your answer in the space provided.

1. What is the main idea of the passage?
   a. Analyzing old air is important because it helps us understand the future and preserve ancient artifacts.
   b. A recent archeological discovery helped us understand the future and the past and introduced new technology.
   c. Archeologists recently discovered a crypt near the Great Pyramid in Egypt, and they carefully examined it.

2. In line 3, what is the purpose of **although?**
   a. It introduces two different ideas.
   b. It introduces two similar ideas.
   c. It introduces two new ideas.

3. In line 6, what is a **crypt?**

   _____

4. In line 7, what is a synonym for **pharaoh?**

   _____

5. Read lines 7 and 8. What is the purpose of the colon (:)?
   a. It shows that the sentence continues for another line.
   b. It connects two sentences and makes them one sentence.
   c. It introduces the purpose of the two boats.

6. In line 10, what does **as** mean?
   a. Before
   b. Like
   c. When

7. In line 11, what does **sealed** mean?
   a. Locked with a key
   b. Closed completely
   c. Hidden carefully

8. Read lines 12–16.
   a. What comes after **in addition**?
      1. More information
      2. The same information
      3. The result of the previous information
   b. What does **chamber** mean?
      1. Crypt
      2. Room
      3. Historian
   c. What does **if so** mean?
      1. If the second chamber really contained a second boat
      2. If archeologists could be sure of the Egyptian custom
      3. If there was really a second chamber next to the crypt

9. In line 18, why is **however** used at the beginning of the paragraph?
   a. To show that the paragraph gives the same information as the paragraph before it
   b. To show that the paragraph gives different information from the paragraph before it

10. Read lines 24–26.
    a. What does **CO₂** represent?
       1. An abbreviation
       2. An amount
       3. A chemical symbol
    b. What is **CO₂**?

       _____

    c. How do you know?

       _____

11. Read lines 29–31. What is the purpose of **in fact?**
    a. To give true information
    b. To emphasize the previous information
    c. To introduce different information

12. Read lines 42 and 43.
    a. What is the purpose of **did** in line 43?
       1. To form a question
       2. To show the past
       3. To give emphasis
    b. What does **confirm** mean?
       1. See
       2. Prove
       3. Write

13. Read lines 44–46. What is the purpose of the colon (:)?
    a. It shows that the sentence continues for another line.
    b. It connects two sentences and makes them one sentence.
    c. It introduces the new nondestructive approach to archeology.

14. Read lines 52 and 53: "New excavations will not only use modern technology, but they will also follow the idea of preserving the entire location for future studies." What is a synonym for **not only . . . but also?**
    a. And
    b. But
    c. So

Information Organization

Read the passage again. Underline what you think are the main ideas. Then scan the reading and complete the following outline, using the sentences that you have underlined to help you. You will use this outline later to answer questions about the reading.

I. Archeological Discovery in Egypt
    A. Date:
    B. Place:
    C. The Discovery:

II. Historians' Belief About Egyptian Burial Customs
    A.
    B. The Purpose of the Boats:

III. The Excavation of the Crypt
    A.
    B.
    C.

IV. What the Archeologists and Historians Hoped to Learn
    A. Information about the Past:
    B. Information about Preserving Wood:
    C. Information about the Future:

V. The Excavation of the Second Chamber
    A. Date:
    B. Method of Excavation:
        1.
        2.
        3.
        4.

VI. The Significance of the Second Excavation
   A.
   B. They practiced a new, nondestructive approach to archeology:
      1.
      2.
      3.
   C. They found out that when the Egyptian government built a museum for the first boat, vibrations from the machinery disturbed the second room and destroyed the seal.

Information Recall and Summary

Read each question carefully. Use your outline to answer the questions. Do not refer back to the passage. When you are finished, write a brief summary of the reading.

1. Where and when did archeologists discover the crypt?

    _____

2. What was the purpose of the crypt?

    _____

3. What is an ancient Egyptian religious custom about death?

    _____

4. Why was the second chamber so important to historians?

    _____

5. How did researchers hope to find answers about the future in the second chamber?

    _____

6. a. Why did it take such a long time before the team opened the second chamber?

        _____

    b. How was the excavation of the second chamber different from the excavation of the first chamber?

        _____

7. How did the air in the second chamber escape?

    _____

    _____

8. What did the team do after they opened and photographed the second chamber?

_____

Summary

Work in pairs or alone. Write a brief summary of the reading, and put it on the blackboard. Compare your summary with your classmates'. Which one best describes the main idea of the reading?

_____

_____

_____

E.   Word Forms

PART 1

In English, verbs change to nouns in several ways. Some verbs become nouns by adding the suffix *-ion* or *-ation*—for example, *preserve (v.)* becomes *preservation (n.)*.

Complete each sentence with the correct form of the words on the left. **Use the correct tense of the verb in either the affirmative or the negative form. Use the singular or plural form of the noun.**

predict *(v.)*
prediction *(n.)*

1. a. The weather forecast _____ snow for last night, but it snowed anyway.
    b. The _____ about the weather was incorrect.

correct *(v.)*
correction *(n.)*

2. a. After our teacher assigns an essay, he always _____ the papers.
    b. If there are only a few _____, the students get good grades.

excavate *(v.)*
excavation *(n.)*

3. a. The _____ of King Tut's tomb was an important and famous event.
    b. Archeologists _____ this tomb in Egypt in the 1920s.

examine *(v.)*
examination *(n.)*

4. a. The doctor's _____ of the sick child will take a long time.
    b. The doctor _____ the sick child until tomorrow to find out what is wrong.

inform *(v.)*
information *(n.)*

5. a. The teacher _____ us about the TOEFL right now.
    b. This _____ will be very helpful to all of us.

In English, verbs change to nouns in several ways. Some verbs become nouns by adding the suffix -y—for example, *embroider (v.)* becomes *embroidery (n.)*.
Complete each sentence with the correct form of the words on the left. **Use the correct tense of the verb in either the affirmative or the negative form. Use the singular or plural form of the noun.**

recover *(v.)*
recovery *(n.)*

1. a. John's boat sank in the middle of a deep lake. However, he _____ it with the help of some friends.
    b. The difficult _____ took several hours.

discover *(v.)*
discovery *(n.)*

2. a. An important _____ that may take place soon is the cure for cancer.
    b. Researchers _____ a cure for cancer in the near future.

deliver *(v.)*
delivery *(n.)*

3. a. The letter carrier _____ the mail early every morning. She comes in the afternoon.
    b. I am excited about the _____ because I am waiting for a letter from my mother.

inquire *(v.)*
inquiry *(n.)*

4. a. When Marla arrived at the airport, she _____ about flights to Paris and to London.
    b. Marla made both _____ at the Information Desk.

master *(v.)*
mastery *(n.)*

5. a. After studying English for four years, Angela finally _____ the language.
    b. Her _____ of English helped her get a higher-paying job.

F. DICTIONARY SKILLS

Read the following sentences. Use the context to help you understand the boldface words. Read the dictionary entry for that word and circle the appropriate definition. Then rewrite the sentence, using the definition you have chosen. Be sure to make your sentence grammatically correct.

1. In 1954, archeologists uncovered an ancient crypt near the **base** of the Great Pyramid.

   base /beɪs/ *n.* **1** the lower part of s.t., foundation. **2** the point where a part of s.t. is connected to the whole. **3** s.t. (a fact, an assumption, etc.) from which a start is made. **4.** the main place where one works or lives, *(syn.)* headquarters.

   _____

   _____

2. The ancient Egyptians had a religious **custom.** They buried their pharaohs with two boats: one to carry the body and the other to carry the soul.

   custom /ˈkʌstəm/ *n.* **1** [C;U] a habitual way of behaving that is special to a person, people, region, or nation. **2** particular way of behaving; habit. **3** regular business given to a firm by its customers. **4** *pl. n.* taxes due to the government on goods imported into a country; import duties.

   _____

   _____

3. The air **escaped** from the second chamber at the time the museum was built for the first boat.

   escape /ɪˈskeɪp/ *v* [I;T] **-caped, -caping, -capes 1** to get away (from prison or another place of confinement). **2** to get free temporarily. **3** to manage to stay free of, to avoid. **4** find a way out; leak.

   _____

   _____

4. The scientists **lowered** a light and a camera into the second chamber.

   lower /ˈloʊər/ *adj. comp of* low—*v.* **1** [T] to let down to a reduced level or position. **2** [I;T] to make less in amount, degree, or intensity. **3 to lower oneself:** to act beneath one's dignity or self-respect.

   _____

   _____

although *(conj.)*	if so	predict *(v.)*
custom *(n.)*	in addition	recover *(v.)*
discovered *(v.)*	in fact	sealed *(adj.)*
excavation *(n.)*		

Read the following sentences. Complete each blank space with the correct word or phrase from the list above. Use each word or phrase only once.

1. _____ I am sick, I can't stay home. I have to go to work anyway.

2. Debbie is doing very well in college. _____, she got 100% on her last five tests and an A+ on her research paper.

3. In the United States, it is a _____ for people to shake hands when they first meet.

4. Today, bottles and cans in stores are carefully _____ to prevent air and germs from getting inside.

5. The supermarket may be open late tonight. _____, I will go shopping after work instead of early tomorrow morning.

6. During the _____ of an old building, construction workers found some ancient artifacts.

7. English students must study grammar. _____, they must study reading, writing, and listening comprehension.

8. Tommy left his sweater in the cafeteria. Fortunately, he was able to _____ it at the Lost and Found Office.

9. Some people go to fortune tellers, who use cards in order to _____ what the future will be.

10. Christopher Columbus _____ America in 1492. Before Columbus found America, most people did not know about its existence.

H. Topics FOR *Discussion* AND *Writing*

1. a. How do archeological discoveries help us understand the past?
    b. Why is understanding the past important?

2. How can the analysis of ancient air be important?

3. a. Do you think it is important not to disturb ancient locations? Why or why not?
    b. Are there times when it is better to remove ancient artifacts and take them to a museum? When?

4. **Write in your journal.** The archeological team left the second boat in the chamber and sealed it again. Do you think it would be better to put the second boat in a museum, too? Why or why not?

I.   Follow-Up Activity

In groups of three or four, form a panel of experts. Someone has discovered the ruins of an ancient city in your country. Your government wants to investigate this site and has asked your panel to plan the excavation. In your group, decide who you will need to help you with this project. Plan the work that your group will do at this location. Decide which artifacts you will take away to a museum and which ones you will leave at the site. When you are finished, compare your plan with your classmates' plans. As a class, decide which plans the government should use.

CHAPTER 10: ANCIENT ARTIFACTS AND ANCIENT AIR

Read the passage below. Fill in the blanks with one word from the list. Use each word only once.

addition	chamber	discovery	however	predict
air	compare	examining	information	recover
although	crypt	excavations	king	sealed
ancient	custom	fact	museum	so

Archeologists made an exciting _____ (1) in Egypt in 1954. During an excavation near the base of the Great Pyramid, they uncovered an ancient crypt. Although they believed that this discovery would help us understand Egypt's past, they also hoped that it would give us important _____ (2) about the future.

This _____ (3) was a tomb, or burial place, for a dead Egyptian pharaoh, or _____ (4). Historians believed that the Egyptians buried their pharaohs with two boats: one to carry the body and another to carry the soul. This was one of their religious customs about death. The archeologists expected to find two boats inside the crypt. As they broke the crypt open, they smelled the scent of wood. The ancient Egyptians had sealed the room so effectively that the aroma of the cedar wood was still preserved. Inside the crypt, archeologists found a 4,600-year-old boat that was in almost perfect condition. In _____ (5), they found another closed room next to the crypt. Archeologists and historians believed that this chamber contained the second boat. If _____ (6), archeologists would have better information about the past. They would be sure about the religious _____ (7) of burying pharaohs with two boats.

_____ (8), this was not the only information they hoped to find. They wondered if the air in the two rooms contained something special that helped to preserve

the wood. This information could help in the preservation of _____ artifacts in
(9)
museums throughout the world. Researchers also hoped to find some answers about the

future by carefully _____ the air in the second chamber. When the
(10)
archeologists opened the first chamber, all the old air escaped. Scientists wanted to

_____ the air in the second chamber, _____ it with the air of the
(11)   (12)
present, and then examine the differences, especially differences in the level of carbon

dioxide (CO_2). This information might help them _____ changes in the air
(13)
in the future. They also did not want outside air to get inside the chamber. Careful

planning would be necessary in order to open the second room and save the air. In

_____, it took years to plan the excavation and to design and make the
(14)
equipment necessary to open the chamber and collect the air inside.

Finally, in October 1986 an international team of scientists, using special equipment,

drilled through the roof of the chamber. The hole they made was kept carefully

_____. As they broke into the ancient room, they realized that the chamber
(15)
was not sealed. They took an air sample. The _____ inside was the same as the
(16)
air outside. Then the team lowered a light and a camera into the small hole and looked at

the interior of the room on a television monitor. The second boat was really there!

After the scientists took samples of the air inside the _____ and
(17)
photographed it completely, they sealed up the hole in the roof and left the room as they

had found it. _____ they did not get samples of 4,600-year-old air, they did
(18)
learn that the Egyptian custom of burying pharaohs with two boats is true. They also

practiced a new, nondestructive approach to archeology: investigate an ancient location,

photograph it, and leave it untouched. When archeologists opened the first chamber, they

removed the boat. The Egyptian government built a _____ on the site for the
(19)
first boat. During the construction of the museum, the vibrations from the heavy machinery

disturbed the second room and probably destroyed the seal. Water leaked in, too, so the

second boat was not as well preserved as the first boat.

The investigation of the second chamber taught archeologists a valuable lesson. New

_____ will not only use modern technology, but they will also follow the idea
(20)

of preserving the entire location for future studies.

How Lunar Eclipses Have Changed History

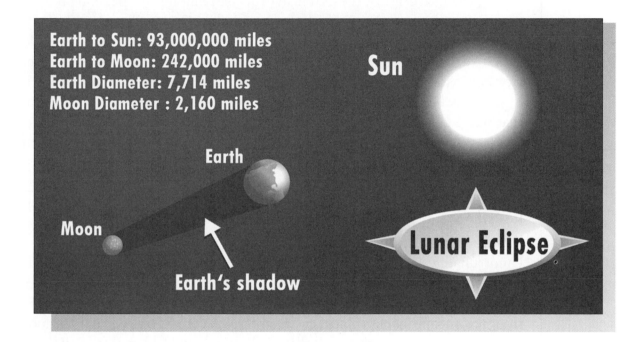

Earth to Sun: 93,000,000 miles
Earth to Moon: 242,000 miles
Earth Diameter: 7,714 miles
Moon Diameter : 2,160 miles

Sun

Earth

Moon

Earth's shadow

Lunar Eclipse

Prereading Preparation

1. Refer to the illustration above. Describe a lunar eclipse.

2. Have you ever seen a lunar eclipse? How does the sky look during a lunar eclipse? What color does the moon appear to be?

3. In the past, some people were superstitious about eclipses. What do you think they believed? Why do you think they were afraid?

1   Lunar eclipses have always fascinated people. Some study eclipses as an
2 astronomical phenomenon; others just enjoy observing their beauty. However, in
3 ancient—and even in more recent—times, lunar eclipses were mysterious,
4 unpredictable, and frightening. In the past, people believed that eclipses were
5 bad omens, or signs, and this superstition has often affected historical events.
6 For instance, a lunar eclipse was partly responsible for the fall of Constantinople
7 in 1453.

8   Constantinople was named for the Roman emperor Constantine, who
9 moved his capital to Byzantium (present-day Istanbul in Turkey) in 324 A.D. The
10 Byzantine government ruled the area for over a thousand years.

11   In the 15th century, the Ottoman (Turkish) Empire was planning to take
12 over Constantinople. The Turkish troops attacked Constantinople in 1402, and
13 again in 1422, but did not succeed. Then in 1451, sultan Mohammed II attacked
14 the city again. Mohammed II had several advantages over the defenders of the
15 city. For instance, he had 250,000 men in the army; Constantinople was fortified
16 by only 7,000 troops. The sultan also had a new style of cannon that shot stones
17 that weighed 1,300 pounds. This weapon was capable of breaking through
18 Constantinople's thick walls. In April 1453, the Turkish army attacked the city's
19 thick walls with its new cannon. The defenders, however, repaired the walls
20 every night. Furthermore, they attacked back several times. Still, after some
21 time, the 7,000 defenders became exhausted. They never thought of giving up,
22 however, because they had faith in an old prophecy. The prediction stated
23 that Constantinople could never fall while the moon was becoming full.
24 Unfortunately, on May 22, 1453, the moon went into an eclipse. The defenders
25 felt frightened and helpless. Three days later, Mohammed II attacked the city
26 again. In a very short time, the Turkish army overpowered Constantinople's
27 troops. Constantinople's defenders had believed the evil omen about the moon;
28 the lunar eclipse made them feel that the battle would be hopeless, and they lost
29 their ability to protect their city from the enemy.

30   A lunar eclipse affected the course of history in Asia, too. According to an
31 ancient Chinese maxim, or saying, each Chinese dynasty starts out when the
32 previous dynasty becomes corrupt, i.e., immoral. This principle is called the
33 Mandate of Heaven because signs in the sky will show that the emperor has
34 become unworthy to rule. The Manchu (Ch'ing) Dynasty in China began its rule
35 in 1644. At first the dynasty was a glorious one, but by the mid 1800s, it had
36 become very corrupt. Finally, in 1851, the Taiping Rebellion took place in order
37 to overthrow the Manchu Dynasty. Some Western powers helped the Manchus
38 try to remain in power. The Manchus also received help from an army of

mercenary[1] soldiers. A British officer named Charles Gordon was a very
successful leader of this mercenary army.

The rebels were defending the city of Soochow, and Gordon's forces were beating them. The rebels' final defense was at the east gate of the city. Gordon decided to make a night attack because there was a full moon and his troops would have enough light to see by. Unfortunately, on the night he chose for his assault there was a lunar eclipse. The Chinese mercenaries interpreted the eclipse as an evil omen, based on the Mandate of Heaven, and felt defeated even before they began to fight. The attack on Soochow was unsuccessful, and a large number of the mercenary soldiers were killed. This battle was Gordon's only loss. Although the mercenaries were unable to take Soochow, the Taiping Rebellion failed, and the Manchu Dynasty remained in power.

Today, scientists can predict lunar eclipses. We no longer fear them as evil omens. However, it is not difficult to understand how, in the past, people believed that eclipses were signs of disaster because they did not understand their true cause.

[1]Mercenaries are men who make money by hiring themselves out as soldiers to anyone who is willing to pay them. They are also called *soldiers of fortune*.

Fact-Finding Exercise

Read the passage again. Read the following statements. Check whether they are True or False. If a statement is false, rewrite the statement so that it is true. Then go back to the passage and find the line that supports your answer.

1. _____ True _____ False   Many people today think that eclipses are bad signs.

   _____

2. _____ True _____ False   Constantinople's defenders failed partly because they thought the eclipse was a bad omen.

   _____

3. _____ True _____ False   In 1851 the Taiping Rebellion overthrew the Manchu Dynasty.

   _____

4. _____ True _____ False   Gordon decided to make a night attack against Soochow because there was an eclipse.

   _____

5. _____ True _____ False   Scientists know when lunar eclipses will occur.

   _____

B.   Reading Analysis

Read each question carefully. Either circle the letter of the correct answer, or write your answer in the space provided.

1. What is the main idea of the passage?
   a. Scientists today can predict lunar eclipses, so people are not afraid of them anymore.
   b. History was affected because people in the past thought lunar eclipses were evil omens.
   c. In 1453, the Turkish army overpowered Constantinople's defenders, and the city fell.

2. In lines 2–4, what is between the dashes (—)?
   a. An example
   b. More information
   c. An explanation

3. Read lines 4 and 5.
   a. In line 5, what is another word for **omen?**

   _____

   b. How do you know?

   _____

   c. In line 5, what is **this superstition?**

   _____

4. a. Read lines 8 and 9. What is the name of **Byzantium** today?

   _____

   b. How do you know?

   _____

5. Read lines 9 and 10: "The Byzantine government ruled the area for over a thousand years."

    a. In this sentence, **ruled** means

        1. fought
        2. governed
        3. defended

    b. In this sentence, **over** means

        1. about
        2. more than
        3. above

6. Read lines 15 and 16. What does **for instance** mean?

    a. For example
    b. As a result
    c. Therefore

7. a. In line 20, what follows **furthermore?**

        1. More information
        2. Examples
        3. An explanation

    b. Complete the following sentence:
        Carol is going to be very busy this summer because she is moving into a new house. Furthermore,

        1. she recently got a new job and must travel a lot for her company.
        2. it is very hot in the summer and she does not like the heat.
        3. she has many friends who are going to help her.

8. a. In line 20, what does **still** mean?

        1. In addition
        2. Even so
        3. Not moving

    b. Complete the following sentence:
        Kelly is very busy with her family, her home, and her job. Still,

        1. she enjoys her job very much
        2. she never takes a vacation in the summer
        3. she always makes time to exercise and eat well

9. Read lines 21–23. What is a synonym for **prophecy?**

   _____

10. a. In line 24, what follows **unfortunately?**
       1. An example
       2. A bad thing
       3. An unbelievable thing
    b. Complete the following sentence:
       Jordan wanted to wake up early in the morning so that he could study for his exam before class. Unfortunately,
       1. his alarm clock didn't ring, and he overslept
       2. he woke up at 6 A.M.
       3. the test was very easy, and he passed it

11. Read lines 30–34.
    a. In line 31, what is a **maxim?**

       _____

    b. How do you know?

       _____

    c. What does **corrupt** mean?

       _____

    d. How do you know?

       _____

    e. What is the **Mandate of Heaven?**

       _____

    f. Why does it have this name?

       _____

12. In line 35, what period of time is the **mid 1800s?**
    a. 1810–1830
    b. 1840–1860
    c. 1860–1880

13. Read lines 36–38.

    a. What does **overthrow** mean?

        1. Replace by force

        2. Defend

        3. Improve

    b. What are Western **powers?**

        1. Forces

        2. Strengths

        3. Countries

14. a. In lines 38 and 39, what are **mercenary soldiers?**

      _____

    b. How do you know?

      _____

    c. This type of information is called a(n)

        1. index

        2. footnote

        3. glossary

C. Information Organization

Read the passage again. Underline what you think are the main ideas. Then scan the reading and complete the following chart, using the sentences that you have underlined to help you. You will use this chart later to answer questions about the reading.

Place	*Constantinople*	*China*
Superstition		
Event and Date		
Result of the Lunar Eclipse		

Information Recall and Summary

Read each question carefully. Use your chart to answer the questions. Do not refer back to the passage. When you are finished, write a brief summary of the reading.

1. What belief did the people of Constantinople have about their city?

   _____

   _____

2. Who attacked Constantinople? When?

   _____

3. a. Who had more men: the defenders of Constantinople or the attacking army?

   _____

   b. Were the defenders successfully defending their city?

   _____

4. What happened after the full moon went into an eclipse on May 22, 1453?

   _____

   _____

   _____

5. What did the Chinese Mandate of Heaven predict?

   _____

   _____

6. What was the purpose of the Taiping Rebellion?

   _____

   _____

7. Why did Gordon lose his only battle in the rebellion?

_____

_____

Summary

Work in pairs or alone. Write a brief summary of the reading, and put it on the blackboard. Compare your summary with your classmates'. Which one best describes the main idea of the reading?

_____

_____

_____

_____

_____

Word Forms

PART 1

In English, adjectives change to nouns in several ways. Some adjectives become nouns by adding the suffix -ity—for example, *individual (adj.)* becomes *individuality (n.)*.

Complete each sentence with the correct form of the words on the left. **Use the singular or plural form of the noun.**

final *(adj.)*
finality *(n.)*

1. a. The judge firmly stated that her decision was _____. She would not change her mind.
    b. She stressed the absolute _____ of her decision by getting up and leaving the courtroom.

unpredictable *(adj.)*
unpredictability *(n.)*

2. a. It is a well-known maxim that the weather is always very _____.
    b. In fact, the only predictable thing about the weather is its _____.

able *(adj.)*
ability *(n.)*

3. a. Jesse has a number of _____.
    b. For example, he is _____ to speak three languages, he knows how to build furniture, and he teaches computer science at the college.

responsible *(adj.)*
responsibility *(n.)*

4. a. As we grow up, we take on more and more _____, especially if we marry and have children.
    b. We become _____ for our family, our job, and our home.

capable *(adj.)*
capability *(n.)*

5. a. Susan is only three years old. She isn't really _____ of riding a bicycle yet.
    b. Her physical _____ are still very limited.

PART 2

In English, nouns change to adjectives in several ways. Some nouns become adjectives by adding the suffix -ous—for example, *danger (n.)* becomes *dangerous (adj.)*.

Complete each sentence with the correct form of the words on the left. **Use the singular or plural form of the noun.**

advantage *(n.)*
advantageous *(adj.)*

1. a. Before deciding to study in the United States, Maria made a list of the _____ and disadvantages of going to college in another country.
   b. She decided that it was more _____ to study abroad than at home.

superstition *(n.)*
superstitious *(adj.)*

2. a. Jack is the most _____ person I've ever met. He won't even go into a building that has a 13th floor.
   b. _____ about lucky and unlucky numbers are cultural. For instance, 13 is not an unlucky number in Japan, but it is in the United States.

mystery *(n.)*
mysterious *(adj.)*

3. a. I received a very _____ package yesterday. When I opened the box, it was empty, and I didn't know who sent it.
   b. I finally solved my little _____ when my sister called and told me she had mailed the box to me.

rebellion *(n.)*
rebellious *(adj.)*

4. a. The people in that country are very _____ because their government is so unjust.
   b. The government has to deal with several _____ every year, and it isn't succeeding.

disaster *(n.)*
disastrous *(adj.)*

5. a. If an earthquake struck our city, it would have _____ results.
   b. This type of _____ would cause hundreds of deaths and injuries.

F. DICTIONARY SKILLS

Read the following sentences. Use the context to help you understand the boldface words. Read the dictionary entry for that word and circle the appropriate definition. Then rewrite the sentence, using the definition you have chosen. Be sure to make your sentence grammatically correct.

1. The fall of Constantinople occurred in 1453. This **event** was of great historical significance.

    > **event** /ɪˈvɛnt/ *n.* **1** a happening, esp. an important one. **2** a competition, contest. **3** an entertainment, gathering.

    _____

    _____

2. An old prophecy predicted that Constantinople could never **fall** while the moon was becoming full.

    > **fall** /fɔl/ *n.* **1** [I] to move suddenly to the ground from a standing position, tumble. **2** [I] to come down from a higher place. **3** *fig.* [I] to suffer a severe loss of status or power. **4** [I] to decline.

    _____

    _____

3. The Byzantine rulers **ruled** over a large area for over a thousand years.

    > **rule** /rul/ *v.* **1** [I;T] to make a society function, to govern, usu. as a king or dictator. **2** [I;T] to decide officially, say what will be done. **3** [T] to draw straight lines on s.t., as with a ruler.

    _____

    _____

4. Lunar eclipses have affected the **course** of history in many countries.

    > **course** /kɔrs/ *n.* **1** a series of lessons in a subject, usu. at a school. **2** an area for sports events. **3** a planned route. **4** a period of time.

    _____

    _____

Vocabulary in Context

affects (v.)	failed (v.)	prophecy (n.)
also (adv.)	maxim (n.)	remains (v.)
attacked (v.)	mysterious (adj.)	still (adv.)
disastrous (adj.)		

Read the following sentences. Complete each blank space with the correct word from the list above. Use each word only once.

1. Gloria _____ to understand Mitch's explanation of the math problem, so she asked Ann to explain it.

2. The effects of last week's storm were _____. Two bridges and 15 buildings were destroyed, and 25 people died.

3. I don't believe the _____ that you can't teach an old dog new tricks.

4. Jan has been studying Russian for three years, but he _____ doesn't understand it very well.

5. It's really true that the weather strongly _____ us. We feel very happy on a clear, sunny day, but we feel depressed on a cold, cloudy day.

6. Cynthia studied full-time at the college last semester. She _____ worked at a full-time job.

7. Our neighbor's dog _____ a burglar in their yard last night. The burglar got away, but he wasn't able to steal anything.

8. I've often heard people tell about the _____ that the world will end, but I don't believe it.

9. Our teacher usually _____ in the room for several minutes after class has ended to answer our questions.

10. A very _____ murder took place in town last week. No one knows who the victim was or why he was killed.

H. Topics FOR Discussion AND Writing

1. Think about a superstition about the sun, planets, and stars that you know about. Describe the superstition and whether it has had good or bad effects on the people/history of your country.

2. Astrologers are people who study the heavens and use the sun, stars, and planets to tell people about their past, present, and future. In a small group, discuss this belief in the effect of the sun, stars, and planets on people's lives. How do you think this belief began?

3. **Write in your journal.** Are you a superstitious person? Write about a superstition that you have.

Follow-Up Activities

1. Even today, many people in different countries have superstitions about the sun, planets, and stars. In small groups, discuss these superstitions in your country and in other countries. Compare your list with your classmates' lists.

Country	Superstitions

2. Most daily newspapers print horoscopes, which predict a person's personality and good or bad luck for that day. Bring a newspaper to class. Each student will read his or her horoscope. Discuss what the horoscope says. Do you believe it? Why or why not? Is the horoscope true for each person with the same "sign?"

3. Solar eclipses (eclipses of the sun) occur throughout the world. Working with a partner, draw an illustration of a solar eclipse. Describe how a solar eclipse takes place.

CHAPTER 11: HOW LUNAR ECLIPSES HAVE CHANGED HISTORY

Read the passage below. Fill in the blanks with one word from the list. Use each word only once.

ability	capable	furthermore	only	take
advantages	eclipses	helpless	prediction	thick
again	enemy	however	repaired	time
attacked	for	omen	succeed	unfortunately

Lunar eclipses have always fascinated people. Some study eclipses as an astronomical phenomenon; others just enjoy observing their beauty. However, in ancient—and even in more recent—times, lunar _____ were mysterious, unpredictable, and
(1)
frightening. In the past, people believed that eclipses were bad omens, or signs, and this superstition has often affected historical events. _____ instance, a lunar eclipse
(2)
was partly responsible for the fall of Constantinople in 1453.

Constantinople was named for the Roman emperor Constantine, who moved his capital to Byzantium (present-day Istanbul in Turkey) in 324 A.D. The Byzantine government ruled the area for over a thousand years.

In the 15th century, the Ottoman (Turkish) Empire was planning to _____
(3)
over Constantinople. The Turkish troops attacked Constantinople in 1402, and
_____ in 1422, but did not _____. Then in 1451, sultan
(4)   (5)
Mohammed II _____ the city again. Mohammed II had several
(6)
_____ over the defenders of the city. For instance, he had 250,000 men in his
(7)
army; Constantinople was fortified by _____ 7,000 troops. The sultan also had
(8)
a new style of cannon that shot stones weighing 1,300 pounds. This weapon was

_____ of breaking through Constantinople's _____ walls. In April
(9)   (10)

1453, the Turkish army attacked the city's thick walls with its new cannon. The defenders,

however, _____ the walls every night. _____, they attacked back
         (11)   (12)

several times. Still, after some _____, the 7,000 defenders became exhausted.
                                 (13)

They never thought of giving up, _____, because they had faith in an old
                                 (14)

prophecy. The _____ stated that Constantinople could never fall while the
              (15)

moon was becoming full. _____, on May 22, 1453, the full moon went into an
                        (16)

eclipse. The defenders felt frightened and _____. Three days later, Mohammed
                                           (17)

II attacked the city again. In a very short time, the Turkish army overpowered

Constantinople's troops. Constantinople's defenders had believed the evil

_____ about the moon; the lunar eclipse made them feel that the battle
(18)

would be hopeless, and they lost their _____ to protect their city from the
                                       (19)

_____.
(20)

12

Mars: Our Neighbor in Space

Prereading Preparation

1. What do you know about the planet Mars?

2. Do you think life exists on Mars today? Why or why not?

3. How can we find out if there is life on Mars?

4. What do you think the surface of Mars is like?

5. What do you think the atmosphere of Mars is like?

Mars: Our Neighbor in Space

Astronomers all over the world were waiting in excitement as August 1993 approached. *Mars Observer*, the American spacecraft, was scheduled to move into orbit around Mars and begin sending new information back to Earth. In addition to mapping the planet, *Mars Observer* was going to study the Martian atmosphere and surface. Unfortunately, scientists lost contact with *Mars Observer* on August 24. The *Mars Observer* mission, which cost $845 million, failed.

In contrast, the United States' previous mission to Mars was a great success. In 1976, two American spacecraft landed on Mars in order to search for signs of life. The tests that the Viking landers performed had negative results. However, scientists still had questions about our close neighbor in space. They wanted to investigate further into the possibility of life on Mars. This was the purpose of the *Mars Observer* mission.

Scientists' interest in the Red Planet is based on an assumption. They believe that 4.5 billion years ago, Mars and Earth began their existence under similar conditions. During the first billion years, liquid water—in contrast to ice—was abundant on the surface of Mars. This is an indication that Mars was much warmer at that time. Mars also had a thicker atmosphere of carbon dioxide (CO_2). Many scientists think it is possible that life began under these favorable conditions. After all, Earth had the same conditions during its first billion years, when life arose. At some point in time, Earth developed an atmosphere that is rich in oxygen, and an ozone layer. Ozone (O_3) is a form of oxygen. The ozone layer protects Earth from harmful ultraviolet light from the sun. While life not only began on Earth, it also survived and became more complex. In contrast, Mars lost its thick atmosphere of carbon dioxide. Ultraviolet radiation intensified. The planet eventually grew colder, and its water froze.

A biologist at NASA (the National Aeronautics and Space Administration), Chris McKay, has suggested three theories about life on Mars. One possibility is that life never developed. A second possibility is that life arose on Mars just as it did on Earth and survived for at least a billion years. The third is that life arose and simple organisms developed. When environmental conditions on Mars changed, life ended.

The two Viking landers performed four experiments. Three experiments tested for biological activity in the soil. However, these tests did not lead to any definite results. The fourth experiment looked for any evidence of life, dead or alive, but found none.

Scientists were dissatisfied with the Viking mission. The two sites where the spacecraft landed provided safe landing places, but they were not particularly interesting locations. Scientists believe there are other areas on Mars that are similar to specific places on Earth that support life. For example,

41 an area in Antarctica, southern Victoria Land, which is not covered by ice,
42 resembles an area on Mars. In the dry valleys of southern Victoria Land, the
43 temperature averages below zero, yet biologists found simple life forms
44 (microorganisms) in rocks and frozen lakes. Perhaps this is also true of places
45 on Mars.

46   Scientists want another investigation of Mars. They want to map the
47 planet's surface and land a spacecraft in a more promising location. They want to
48 search for fossils, the ancient remains of life. If life ever existed on Mars,
49 scientists believe that future missions might find records of it under sand, or in
50 the ice. They are very disappointed in the failure of the *Mars Observer* mission and
51 want to start a new mission. Other countries are interested in Mars, too. For
52 example, Russia is also planning to send an unmanned spacecraft to Mars in the
53 near future.

54   Even if future missions discover no evidence of past or present life on Mars,
55 scientists will look for the answers to other, intriguing questions. How is Earth
56 different from Mars? How can we explain the development of life here on our
57 planet and not on Mars, our close neighbor? Are we alone in the universe?

Fact-Finding Exercise

Read the passage again. Read the following statements. Check whether they are True or False. If a statement is false, rewrite the statement so that it is true. Then go back to the passage and find the line that supports your answer.

1. ____ True ____ False   *Mars Observer* was successful in 1993.

   _____

2. ____ True ____ False   The 1976 Viking mission to Mars was successful.

   _____

3. ____ True ____ False   Mars and Earth were very similar 4.5 billion years ago.

   _____

4. ____ True ____ False   Scientists believe there is liquid water on Mars now.

   _____

5. ____ True ____ False   The two Viking landers performed three experiments.

   _____

6. ____ True ____ False   The spacecraft landed at two safe but uninteresting places.

   _____

7. ____ True ____ False   Scientists believe they may find ancient remains of life on Mars under sand or in ice.

   _____

8. ____ True ____ False   Russia may send a spacecraft to Mars.

   _____

Read each question carefully. Either circle the letter of the correct answer, or write your answer in the space provided.

1. What is the main idea of the passage?
   a. NASA biologists have three possible theories about life on Mars.
   b. The United States sent two missions to Mars, but one was unsuccessful.
   c. Scientists are interested in the possibility that there is or was life on Mars.

2. The author of this article is in favor of sending more spacecraft to Mars.
   a. Yes
   b. No
   c. We don't know

3. Read lines 2–5.
   a. How many tasks was *Mars Observer* going to perform?
      1. One
      2. Two
      3. Three
   b. How do you know?

   _____

4. Read lines 7 and 8.
   a. What does **in contrast** indicate?
      1. Two similar ideas
      2. Two opposite ideas
   b. Which two words show this relationship?

   _____

5. In line 10, what does **our close neighbor in space** refer to?

   a. The spacecraft

   b. Mars

   c. The sun

6. In line 13, what does **the Red Planet** refer to?

   a. The sun

   b. Earth

   c. Mars

7. Read lines 13–15. Which of the following statements is true?

   a. Mars is older than Earth.

   b. Earth is older than Mars.

   c. Mars and Earth are the same age.

8. Read lines 15 and 16. "During the first billion years, liquid water—in contrast to ice—was abundant on the surface of Mars."

   a. What form does the water on Mars have today?

      1. Liquid

      2. Solid

   b. How do you know?

   _____

9. In lines 17–18 and in line 21, what do CO_2 and O_3 represent?

   a. Chemical symbols

   b. Abbreviations

   c. Amounts

10. a. In line 27, what is in parentheses?

      1. An abbreviation

      2. The purpose of NASA

      3. The words that NASA stands for

    b. Why do you think **NASA** is used in the sentence, and **National Aeronautics and Space Administration** is in parentheses?

    _____

11. In lines 34 and 35, what does **definite** indicate?
    a. Certainty
    b. Uncertainty

12. In lines 37–40, which three words are synonyms of **sites?**

    _____

13. Read lines 42–44. What does **yet** mean?
    a. But
    b. And
    c. So

14. a. In line 44, what are **microorganisms?**

    _____

    b. Why is **microorganisms** in parentheses?
       1. It is an example.
       2. It is a special word.
       3. It is a foreign word.

15. Read lines 47 and 48.
    a. What are **fossils?**

    _____

    b. How do you know?

    _____

Information Organization

Read the passage again. Underline what you think are the main ideas. Then scan the reading and complete the following outline, using the sentences that you have underlined to help you. You will use this outline later to answer questions about the reading.

I. *Mars Observer* Mission

    A. Date:

    B. Purpose: to move into orbit around Mars and send new information back to Earth

        1.

        2.

    C. Outcome:

II.

    A. Date:

    B. Purpose:

    C. Outcome:

III. Data about Mars and Earth

    A. Age of Mars and Earth:

    B. Water on Mars and Earth:

    C. Conditions on Mars:

    D. Life on Earth:

        Life on Mars:

    E. Earth's Atmosphere:

        Mars's Atmosphere:

IV. Three Theories about Life on Mars

    A.

    B.

    C.

V. The Viking Landers Experiments
    A. Three Experiments:
    B. The Fourth Experiment:
    C. Results of all Four Experiments:

VI. Why Scientists Want to Investigate Mars Again
    A.
    B. They want to search for fossils.

VII. Questions That Scientists Want to Answer
    A.
    B.
    C.

D.　Information Recall and Summary

Read each question carefully. Use your outline to answer the questions. Do not refer back to the passage. When you are finished, write a brief summary of the reading.

1. In the beginning, how were Earth and Mars similar?

   _____

   _____

2. How did Earth and Mars become different?

   _____

3. Describe the three theories about life on Mars.

   a. _____

   _____

   b. _____

   _____

   c. _____

   _____

4. a. What tests did the Viking landers perform on Mars?

   _____

   b. What were the results of these tests?

   _____

5. Why do scientists believe that there are other areas on Mars that may support life?

_____

6. What do scientists want to learn in the future?

_____

Summary

Work in pairs or alone. Write a brief summary of the reading, and put it on the blackboard. Compare your summary with your classmates'. Which one best describes the main idea of the reading?

_____

_____

_____

_____

_____

E. Word Forms

PART 1

In English, nouns change to adjectives in several ways. Some nouns become adjectives by adding the suffix *-al*—for example, *person (n.)* becomes *personal (adj.)*

Complete each sentence with the correct form of the words on the left. **Use the singular or plural form of the noun.**

experiment *(n.)*
experimental *(adj.)*

1. a. The design for a car that operates on solar energy is in the _____ stage.
   b. Researchers will need to perform dozens of _____ to perfect this car.

environment *(n.)*
environmental *(adj.)*

2. a. Life can survive in hostile _____, such as the black depths of the oceans.
   b. When _____ conditions change radically, some life forms die out.

development *(n.)*
developmental *(adj.)*

3. a. There are specialists in the field of psychology called _____ psychologists.
   b. These people study the complex _____ of humans from birth to death.

accident *(n.)*
accidental *(adj.)*

4. a. There was a fatal _____ at the factory yesterday.
   b. The _____ explosion of a gas tank caused the deaths of three people.

function *(n.)*
functional *(adj.)*

5. a. The governor announced that the new power plant will be _____ by next week.
   b. It will serve an important _____ as an extra source of energy.

In English, adjectives change to verbs in several ways. Some adjectives change to verbs by adding the suffix *-ify*—for example, *solid (adj.)* becomes *solidify (v.)*.

Complete each sentence with the correct form of the words on the left. **Use the correct tense of the verb in either the affirmative or the negative form.**

intense *(adj.)*
intensify *(v.)*

1. a. A storm arose on the ocean and _____ in severity. The captain of the ship became worried.
   b. He overcame his _____ feeling of fear and organized the crew to try to save the ship.

simple *(adj.)*
simplify *(v.)*

2. a. The college application form is not _____ enough, and many applicants fill it out incorrectly.
   b. As a result, the Admissions Office _____ the form in time for next term's applicants.

specific *(adj.)*
specify *(v.)*

3. a. Jeff is writing a beginner's cookbook, so his directions must be quite _____.
   b. If he _____ exactly what to do, many beginners will become very frustrated.

clear *(adj.)*
clarify *(v.)*

4. a. Because the salesperson _____ the directions, Judy couldn't start up her new computer.
   b. She called the manufacturer, who sent an expert to give Judy _____ instructions, and she was able to begin working.

pure *(adj.)*
purify *(v.)*

5. a. When Fay and Ken go camping in the mountains next summer, they will not have any _____ water to drink.
   b. They _____ the water they find by boiling it for 20 minutes.

F. DICTIONARY SKILLS

Read the following sentences. Use the context to help you understand the boldface words. Read the dictionary entry for that word and circle the appropriate definition. Then rewrite the sentence, using the definition you have chosen. Be sure to make your sentence grammatically correct.

1. Scientists lost **contact** with *Mars Observer* on August 24.

> **contact** /ˈkɑnˌtækt/ *n.* **1** [U] touch. **2** [C] a person one knows, esp. who can get s.t. done. **3** [C] an electrical point. **4** communication with s.o.

_____

_____

2. The spacecraft landed on Mars in order to search for any **signs** of life.

> **sign** /saɪn/ *n.* **1** a board or poster with information on it. **2** an action or other non-spoken way of communicating. **3** a symbol. **4** something that gives evidence, points to the existence or probability of something: *Are dark clouds a ~ of rain?*

_____

_____

3. Scientists searched the rocks and frozen lakes of Antarctica. They found life forms that were **simple.** They hope to find such life forms on Mars.

> **simple** /ˈsɪmpəl/ *adj.* **1** without many details, not complex. **2** easy to do. **3** ordinary, pure. **4** not able to think in a complicated way.

_____

_____

4. Scientists want to land a spacecraft in a location that has more **promise** than the previous landing sites.

> **promise** /ˈprɑmɪs/ *n.* [C;U] **1** a commitment. **2** [U] **to hold** or **have promise:** to show signs or hope that s.t. good will result.

_____

_____

abundant *(adj.)*	investigate *(v.)*	support *(v.)*
arise *(v.)*	perform *(v.)*	survive *(v.)*
assumption *(n.)*	similar *(adj.)*	theory *(n.)*
intriguing *(adj.)*		

Read the following sentences. Complete each blank space with the correct word from the list above. Use each word only once.

1. A human being can _____ without food or water for several days, but will die within moments without air.

2. The police always _____ murders and robberies to try to find out who committed the crimes so they can arrest them.

3. Water is _____ in many places, but it is rare in deserts.

4. In 1916, an astronomer named Percival Lowell had a _____ that there was a ninth planet, but Pluto was not discovered until 1930.

5. When Pat opened a letter from the college she had applied to, she began to cry. Susan was watching her and made the _____ that the news was bad. Her guess was correct: Pat was not accepted by the college.

6. Many students do not _____ well on examinations because they become very nervous and tense.

7. Fay suggested a two-month camping trip to the Himalayas next summer. Her husband Ken thought the idea was _____. They had never done anything so exciting before!

8. Venus and Earth are _____ in size. However, the surface temperature of Venus is 600 degrees Fahrenheit!

9. It is probably impossible for life to ever _____ on Venus because of its intense surface heat.

10. Maria will attend college next semester, and her parents agreed to _____ her, so she will not have to get a job.

H. Topics FOR Discussion AND Writing

1. Do you think that life on Earth is simply an accident? Why or why not?

2. Do you think it is important for scientists to study other places in space? Explain your answer.

3. Does your country have a space program? If so, how would you compare it to the space program in this country?

4. **Write in your journal.** Do you think there is life on another planet? Why or why not?

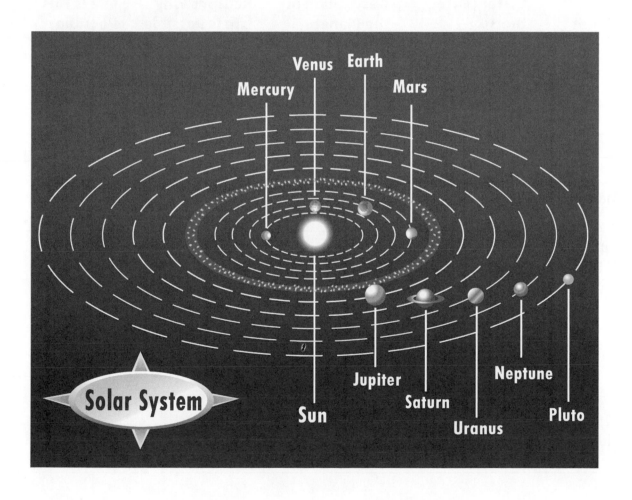

Follow-Up Activity

Choose a planet in our solar system to read about. Prepare a report on the planet. Use the chart below to record your information. In class, work in groups of three. Discuss the planets you have chosen. Decide whether it is possible for life to exist on these planets. List your reasons. Compare your information with your classmates' information. As a class, decide which planets could possibly support life.

Planet	Diameter and Distance from the Sun	Description of the Planet	Reasons Why Life Is Possible	Reasons Why Life Is Not Possible
Mercury				
Venus				
Earth				
Mars				
Jupiter				
Saturn				
Uranus				
Neptune				
Pluto				

Cloze Quiz

CHAPTER 12: MARS: OUR NEIGHBOR IN SPACE

Read the passage below. Fill in the blanks with one word from the list. Use each word only once.

abundant	contrast	intriguing	planet	support
arose	experiments	investigation	possibility	survived
assumption	fossils	locations	protects	theories
conditions	intensified	performed	similar	unfortunately

Astronomers all over the world were waiting in excitement as August 1993 approached. *Mars Observer,* the American spacecraft, was scheduled to move into orbit around Mars. In addition to mapping the _____ , *Mars Observer* was going to (1) study the Martian atmosphere and surface. _____ , scientists lost contact with (2) *Mars Observer* on August 24.

In _____ , the United States' previous mission to Mars in 1976 was a great (3) success. Two American spacecraft landed on Mars in order to search for signs of life. The tests that the Viking landers _____ had negative results. However, scientists (4) still had questions about Mars. They wanted to investigate further into the _____ of life on Mars. (5)

Scientists' interest in the Red Planet is based on an _____ . They believe (6) that 4.5 billion years ago, Mars and Earth began their existence under _____ (7) conditions. During the first billion years, liquid water was _____ on the surface (8) of Mars. This is an indication that Mars was much warmer at that time. Mars also had a thicker atmosphere of carbon dioxide (CO_2). Many scientists think it is possible that life began under these favorable conditions. After all, Earth had the same conditions during its first billion years, when life _____ . At some point in time, Earth developed an (9) atmosphere that is rich in oxygen, and an ozone layer. The ozone layer _____ (10) Earth from harmful ultraviolet light from the Sun. While life not only began on Earth, it also

_____ (11) and became more complex. In contrast, Mars lost its thick atmosphere of carbon dioxide. Ultraviolet radiation _____ (12). The planet grew colder, and its

water froze.

A biologist at NASA, Chris McKay, has suggested three _____ (13) about life on Mars. One possibility is that life never developed. A second possibility is that life arose during the first billion years, but did not survive. The third is that life arose and simple organisms developed. When environmental _____ (14) on Mars changed, life ended.

The two Viking landers performed four _____ (15). Three experiments tested for biological activity in the soil. The fourth experiment looked for evidence of life. All the tests were negative.

Scientists were dissatisfied because the two sites where the Viking spacecraft landed provided safe landing places, but they were not particularly interesting _____ (16). Scientists believe there are other areas on Mars that are similar to specific places on Earth that _____ (17) life. For example, an area in Antarctica, southern Victoria Land, which is not covered by ice, resembles an area on Mars. In its dry valleys, the temperature in southern Victoria Land averages below zero, yet biologists found simple life forms. Perhaps this is also true of places on Mars.

Scientists want another _____ (18) of Mars. They want to map the planet's surface and land a spacecraft in a more promising location. They want to search for

_____ (19), the ancient remains of life. If life ever existed on Mars, scientists believe that future missions might find records of it.

Even if future missions discover no evidence of past or present life on Mars, scientists will look for the answers to other, _____ (20) questions. How is Earth different from Mars? How can we explain the development of life here on our planet and not on Mars, our close neighbor? Are we alone in the universe?

Unit 4 Review

K.　Crossword Puzzle

Crossword Puzzle Clues

Across

2. A sign

4. You will succeed _____ you work hard.

6. Ask for information

7. Surroundings; everything around you

11. I am going _____ eat lunch

12. Habit; usual behavior

13. Room

14. Soldier of fortune

17. I am _____ tired. I slept very well last night.

19. Good, better; bad, _____

21. An Egyptian king

23. I am; we _____.

24. The past tense of **make**

25. Unluckily

26. To learn very well; to become skilled at something

28. The past tense of **sit**

31. A test

34. The past tense of **have**

35. Certainly; surely

37. An unproven idea

Down

1. Find
2. To take over by force
3. The opposite of **yes**
5. In addition; moreover
8. This coat costs $2,000. It is _____ expensive.
9. A simple life form
10. Burial place
15. Dig up
16. An _____ is a person who studies the sun, planets, and stars.
18. The opposite of **down**
20. A belief
22. My, his, _____
27. Not complex
29. Tightly closed
30. The opposite of **succeed**
32. The opposite of **difficult**
33. This, that, _____, those
36. The opposite of **no**

UNIT 4 DISCUSSION

1. The three chapters in this unit discuss the uses of technology in solving problems related to the past, the present, and the future. What do you think are the most important problems science and modern technology should try to solve?

2. What can the past teach us about the present? How can this help us in the future?

3. How does technology help us today? Give specific examples.

1. What do you know about the planet Mars? Does life exist there now? Do you think simple life forms existed on Mars in the past?

2. Read the statements. Then watch the video once or twice. Check (√) the correct answer.

   a. The blue and purple spots on the planet indicate the presence of _____.

   ____ oxygen   ____ hydrogen
   ____ carbon dioxide   ____ many gases

   b. How deep underground is the water ice? _____

   ____ 1–2 feet   ____ 2–3 feet   ____ 3–4 feet   ____ 4–5 feet

   c. It is possible that Mars had liquid water on the surface when its temperature was_____.

   ____ colder   ____ darker   ____ warmer   ____ lighter

   d. The NASA scientist believes that the hydrogen is so _____ in the north and south that it is a definite sign of water ice.

   ____ scarce   ____ abundant   ____ insignificant   ____ hard

   e. One scientist is intrigued because we may soon know the answer to the question "Are we _____?"

   ____ similar   ____ fossils   ____ in contrast   ____ alone

3. Do you think Mars will ever be a stopover point for space explorers? Will people in spacecraft investigate other planets in the future?

Surfing THE **INTERNET**

Enter the key words "Mars" or "lunar eclipse" into a search engine. Find a good photograph and some interesting information about Mars or the Earth's moon and write down the website to share with a partner.

Optional Activity: Go to the NASA.gov website to search for more information about the planet Mars or lunar eclipses. Share what you've learned or what you've seen with a partner or your class. What else can you find on that website? Explain new vocabulary about space or space exploration.

INDEX OF KEY WORDS AND PHRASES

SKILLS INDEX